WORSHIP:

Good News In Action

EDITED BY MANDUS A. EGGE

Joseph A. Sittler
Henry E. Horn
James F. White
Jaroslav Pelikan
Eugene L. Brand
Edward A. Sovik
Daniel B. Stevick
Wayne E. Saffen

AUGSBURG PUBLISHING HOUSE
MINNEAPOLIS, MINNESOTA

WORSHIP: GOOD NEWS IN ACTION

Copyright © 1973 Augsburg Publishing House

Library of Congress Catalog Card No. 73-88598

International Standard Book No. 0-8066-1402-1

Scripture quotations unless otherwise noted are from the Revised Standard Version of the Bible, copyright 1946 and 1952 by the Division of Christian Education of the National Council of Churches, and are used by permission.

Manufactured in the United States of America.

Contents

Preface

When the Inter-Lutheran Commission on Worship began its work in the late sixties, it stated its goals in part as follows:

The commission expects to produce a new, common liturgy and hymnal for the churches. It is concerned that the richness of the tradition be retained; at the same time it seeks to enhance and enliven that tradition with lively speech and songs for the church of the future.

To that end the commission is engaged in preparing materials that are provisional in nature. . . .

By 1973 many of the provisional materials were ready, among them an order for the celebration of the Eucharist with four musical settings, six seasonal Services of the Word, two forms for the Order of Marriage, and two booklets of new hymns. Some of these items have been in use in congregations for two to five years. In addition, a new lectionary and calendar for the church year were ready, and other orders were almost ready for the publishers. It seemed to the commissions on worship of the church bodies involved in this work that the time had come for a major conference on worship.

There is today a changing mood in regard to worship—some call it liturgical renewal, others a revolution in worship. Whatever one might call it, there is a real desire on the part of leaders of worship, both clergy and lay, for a revitalization of worship. Language continues to change, and the antiquated language used in worship in most Protestant churches must be updated if it is to speak to today's people. Music changes, too, and some people have become tired of some of the tunes that have been sung for decades and even centuries.

Four Lutheran church bodies, the Lutheran Church in America, The American Lutheran Church, The Evangelical Lutheran Church of Canada, and The Lutheran Church—Missouri Synod, together with the Lutheran Society for Worship, Music and the Arts therefore agreed that they would jointly hold a conference on worship. The conference was held in Minneapolis, Minnesota on June 11-15, 1973.

In planning the program for the conference, an attempt was made to involve every art used in worship. Following the keynote address, seven lectures were presented simultaneously, dealing with various aspects of worship. Fifty-two seminars and workshops followed the addresses, together with a substantial number of concerts and dramatic presentations. Six services were held, three of them being celebrations of the Eucharist.

"Good News in Action" was the theme of the conference, and hence the title of this book which includes the eight lectures.

Dr. Joseph Sittler, of the Divinity School, University of Chicago, was the keynoter, a role he has fulfilled adequately in many conferences. His theme was "Dogma and Doxa." The seven lectures which introduced sub-topics in the conference program were given by outstanding theologians and scholars. "Worship: The Gospel in Action" was presented out of a university background because Dr. Henry E. Horn ministers to students at Harvard University and other institutions of higher education in the Boston area. A Methodist, Dr. James F. White of Perkins School of Theology and author of an excellent book, *New Forms of Worship*, spoke on "Worship in Our Changing Culture." Dr. Jaroslav Pelikan is a church historian, well-known in theological circles for his writings and his lectures, hence his theme, "Worship Between Yesterday and Tomorrow." Worship forms are in constant need of being updated; therefore Dr. Eugene Brand discussed "New

Accents in Baptism and the Eucharist." Dr. Brand was chairman of the committee which prepared the new Lutheran order for the celebration of Holy Communion. Architects have been in the forefront in liturgical renewal, and one of the leaders in architectural design for worship centers is Mr. Edward A. Sovik. His topic was "The Place of Worship: Environment for Action." "Renewing the Language of Worship" is a constant need for Christian people, both the spoken language and the acted, symbolic language. Dr. Daniel B. Stevick (Episcopal) introduced this subject. Is there a relationship between Christianity and politics? Yes, said the Reverend Wayne Saffen in his lecture on "Worship and Political Responsibility."

At least one hundred people were involved in planning and directing the conference, but those directly in charge included Charles Anders, conference manager, and the members of the steering committee, Paul Bosch, Eugene Brand, Daniel Brockopp, E. Theo. DeLaney, David Lindblom, Alf Romstad, Warren Rubel, Ralph Van Loon and the undersigned.

It is the hope and prayer of this committee that the published lectures, as the conference itself, will assist the leaders of worship in all churches in making worship central in every congregation and meaningful to every worshiper, to the glory of him who is the head of the Church, Jesus Christ, our Savior and Lord.

Mandus A. Egge, Chairman
Conference on Worship Steering Committee

Minneapolis, Minnesota
June 1973

Joseph A. Sittler

Dogma and Doxa

The task I have been asked to undertake has been announced as a keynote address. The usual associations of that term do not suggest the kind of reflection appropriate to the issue before us. The situation that brings us together is in such a state of confusion that a keynote address in the common usage of that term could only be prepared by a vehement act of forgetfulness!

Political conventions begin with a keynote address. The purpose of that address is to summarize what is perfectly clear to all loyal members of the party, to point with pride to past accomplishments and view with alarm the behavior of the party one hopes to supplant. Such an address is a rhetorical articulation of the obvious, a precise guide to the course of action that shall save the nation, and a resounding summons to the troops to take up arms against a sea of troubles, and, by opposing, end them.

There is, however, another and better interpretation of the function of the opening address at a convocation addressed to a common interest—and I shall state what that is and do what I can to advance it. A key is meant to turn a lock, and by that action permit access to something. Such an action is necessary, definite, clear—but limited. Let me, for a moment, speak of the limits of it, and thus specify what this keynote will not do, and serve notice of what it will attempt.

7

I shall not expound upon the crisis in the culture and the impact of that upon Christian worship. What needs to be said at this point is well summarized in a single citation. In September of 1972 five hundred members of British and Irish churches met for ten days to consider the crises that confront Christianity today. John Macquarrie, summarizing the findings of one of the eight commissions, said, "The state of the Church, we believe, is better described as bewilderment rather than skepticism . . . things are happening so fast and landmarks disappearing so swiftly that people are suffering from unprecedented emotional stress. . . ." *(Tempo,* N.C.C. Newsletter, April, 1973).

In North America the state of affairs is not only comparable; it is perhaps more acute. Both cultures exhibit a fatigue of two centuries of industrial-technological adjustments of the human spirit. One could use this hour to construct a mordant symphony out of the many voices—reportorial, analytical and strident—which are presently adding data to Professor Macquarrie's statement. But an accumulation of lamentations would not be useful. The content and the force of these is already known to you. That knowledge, in fact, is why you are here. I am moved to add that such detailed reports of the demolition of structures, while admirable and necessary work, is also often a favorite ploy of the learned whereby at one and the same time they exhibit their knowledge and evade the constructive requirements of the moment. History can become the most honorable refuge of the disengaged. I recall the self-absolving comment of a onetime colleague who regularly excused himself from flinty problems with the remark "I am content to repose upon the broad bosom of the historical!"

So much, then, for reportage and for lamentation.

Discerning a Process of Solidification

Let us turn, now, to the constructive task of this paper. I do that by asking a large and exceedingly complex question. Is it possible to discern, among the many and tumultuous movements, issues, demolitions and reconstructions that have characterized Christian theological reflection since World War I any process of solidification? Is it possible to discern amidst the swirling energies of sixty years of historical, critical, reformulative studies—biblical, systematic, methodological—any centers of concern that are becoming persistent and steady, that give promise of the kind of pattern that one sees in an astronomer's photograph of the night sky, with some constellations showing a density that sets them off from the spangled vastness of the whole?

I think there are such constellations a-forming in our time, and I shall try to name them and ask after their meaning and possible guidance for the future of Christian worship. In making such an effort I am vividly conscious of the limits, perspectival, personal and substantial that inhere in such an effort. Such awareness serves indeed to sober us; but given the bewilderment I have alluded to, it dare not paralyze us. So, then, to the job.

A. Eschatology

The first area in which I think one can see a "process of solidification" is around the venerable theme—*eschatology*.

Albert Schweitzer's *Quest for the Historical Jesus* at the beginning of the century, must ever be regarded as one of the turnings in a new direction in the long history of historical-biblical study. For the fundamental affirmation of that work, then so brash and unsettling, has long since become the operating presupposition of an entire discipline. The life-world, the thought-world, the spiritually-envisioned world of Jesus, and indeed the entire testimony to him in the first century, was radically eschatological. By "eschatological" Schweitzer meant, and we still mean, a sense of the boundedness, the pathos and promise of historical life under and within the brackets of the powers of the divine life, however these are manifested and apprehended.

This strange—and to contemporary popular ideas of linear unfolding toward infinite fulfilments of historical forms and vitalities—even esoteric ways of living in, beholding, and assessing the world drenches the fundamental Christian mind with a very particular mood and fixes it in a very particular stance. All experiences, all interpretations of the past, all expectations of the future, all assessments and uses of the present, all images, terms, elements and forms of worship are interiorly determined by this center of vision. Every place as particular is relativized by eschatology (neither on this mountain nor in Jerusalem); every time is relativized (you know neither the times nor the seasons); every human sense of limit is made questionable (exceeding more than you ask or think); and every ideal human boundlessness is brought up sharp (my strength is perfected in weakness).

A summary statement of the Christian way of being-in-the-world is literally a new horizon for all contemplation, faith and action. That new horizon underlies the paradoxical structure and fabric of the Christian life—life in death and death in life; bear ye one another's burdens—every man must bear his own burden —cast your burden upon the Lord. This is utter nonsense except in an eschatological context. This horizon constitutes the strange activity within historical boundedness which would, humanly, be annihilated by inexorable limit. But Christian faith within history is not annihilated! For every active verb has its roots deep sunk in the ineffable passive. The active verb *to know* is both qualified by and released from its qualification by the passive "I have been known." The active verb *to love* is both qualified and redeemed from its failures by the "I have been loved." Every impetus and limitation of *I will* is both acknowledged, commended and redeemed from its human febrility by the mighty passive verbs—for God has promised, determined, willed.

This eschatological mode of existence alone explains what were otherwise incomprehensible: an *active* passivity, ethically absolute commands delivered to relative capacities, discouragement borne without despair, men cast down but not destroyed. But the purposes of this conference will not be sufficiently served if the eschatological is affirmed to be the formative mode and horizon of only early Christian life and thought. I would venture the judgment that this way of man's being in the world has so permeated and tinctured all historical life in the West—persisted, even if unacknowledged or unaware—that the very story and substance of Western culture would not be the thing it is save for this strange boundless within the humanly bounded.

There is much data, old and new, which someone more learned than I could summon to that judgment; but I shall summon only so much as I can warrant by tested experience. For seventeen years I have had a marginal but active relation to the discipline that is named in my school 'Theology and Literature.' For such a field of study to be legitimized within a university that has other and large faculties whose subject matter is the substance and meaning of man's achievements in imaginative literature entails a defense of this discipline within a theological faculty. When the question is urged, as it regularly is, why a faculty of Divinity should presume to duplicate researches properly central to others, one must give a conceptually clear and persuasive answer. And because a probing for a reply to that question discloses so clearly what I have affirmed to be the permeative and formative power of the eschatological, I ask leave to expand somewhat upon it.

Let us suppose that we are reading a text that aspires to be a genuine encounter with reality (solemn or trivial, epic or simply entertaining). The text rests its claim to attention upon its effort to speak of how things are with the endless drama of the human. As we read are we not aware of a question that lurks behind and hovers over what we are doing? Behind such obvious matters as style, situation, plot, organization, employment of symbols and all the other stratagems of the writer, one wants to know, perhaps without articulating the query, "What's going on here?" What "arrow of thought," to use Professor Paul Ricoeur's phrase, is being launched, what sense for the reality and truth of life, what world-understanding and self-understanding or feeling am I being invited to accredit, share, and even participate in? That question does not, to be sure, impede the forward movement of the story, or manifestly tug us to a halt as we read. But that question haunts reflection when the reading is finished; that question must be surfaced and given a reply if one is even to make a judgment that one book is better than another!

The unexpungeable question may be called by literary critics an illicit one; but the stubborn human will not thereby put it aside as of no significance. In this quality of stubbornness the question is like the conscience; each man's conscience has indeed its particular history and its individual sensibility. But the force of conscience is not annuled, or its gravity thereby abated.

When I ask "What's going on here?" I am actually engaged in a judgment of worth, of truth, of the moral, of the good that in all life is to be sought, of the evil that is always to be discerned and avoided. Literature, whether consciously so or not, is a report about, a partner to, a tactic of that seeking. It is a probing and an uncovering, an unfolding toward judgment. The work of imaginative literature punctures as it probes; it traces out the involuted layers of the devices men use to mask or to silence ambiguity. And it gropes for a language which shall release without distortion the truth of things—a truth which exists apart from language but which it is a function of language to give "a local habitation and a name."

If, then, the moral, the good, the what-ought-to-be envisioned and done is the fundamental norm of literature—we can now bring this fact into intersection with all we have said about the eschatological. For the general human concern with the moral has been creatively complicated, given profound new dimensions by the terms and symbols of the Christian story. And that piercing of the western moral soul and culture by this specifically Christian event is so powerful and pervasive a component in western culture that understanding and our sense for reality is radically diminished by its excision.

I have no intention, nor indeed the time, to expound or fully illustrate this claim for all the large symbols of the faith. But that the eschatological sense for life, history and reality has exercised this force, and that at this moment is doing so in fresh terms I have no doubt at all. The eschatological as the Christian pre-understanding of the nature of things has no equivalent in all the data of the history of religions as such. It can therefore with justice be postulated as a unique component in western culture which it is the duty of a theological criticism to recognize and employ as men seek for truth and reality. From Dostoevsky's Sonya and Ivan and Aloysha to Mark Twain's Huck Finn; from Hawthorne and Melville to Henry James; from Robert Penn Warren's play about Thomas Jefferson's morally complicated conscience to Dorothy Parker's morally ironic little jingles, the literature of the west cannot tear itself loose from the twin pathos and allure of an exploration of the moral as that moral quest has been complicated by the eschato-logical.

Such a literature exists where there has been a Christian tradition; such a literature has not existed and does not presently exist where that tradition has not been. Nor do our present confusions about the institutional, propositional, liturgical transmitters of that tradi-tion seem likely to dislodge the truth-firm density of the terrible moral from the reflective life of our culture. That very confusion seems rather to affirm it. And while the wings of Jonathan Living-ston Seagull may not be the solidest organs to probe it with, our generation has forged tougher ones—the dramatists Beckett and Arthur Miller, the poets Berryman, Roethke, and Wilbur, the novel-ists Updike and Bellow. How strange that just at the time when both celebrative liturgies and parish preaching seem to have lost the profundity of the eschatological and settled for a combination of sheer affirmation and moralization, the most sensitive artists of our time are both recovering and re-exploring it.

There is a second force at work to call the mind of this genera-tion to the reality that tradition has known as the eschatological. It is the present communication to the popular mind of what the earth-sciences have always known—that the seeming tough life of the earth is bound into a delicate system by a million threads of inter-relatedness; that assumptions of inexhaustible resources and energies is a fateful illusion; that finitude is a cosmic fact before it is personal knowledge; that beginning, maturing, ending, or radical transformation is in the structure of things and not only a phenom-enon of sentient life; that a kind of natural "judgment" is built into the natural-actual as well as to the personal-historical. Ecolog-ical fact is but the eschatological operating as nature!

The growing knowledge that man's life is bound into the inter-calated bundle of all that is, and the power of this knowledge deeply to transform man's thinking about himself, the universe, and God it is not yet possible to assess, and we must be careful not to overestimate its transformative force. For the historical evidence of man's undeterred ability to "suppress the truth in unrighteousness" is formidable. That this and following generations, clutching acquisitiveness and concupiscence to their affluent breasts have the moral possibility to march straight into damnation with open eyes is a mordant prospect. But the ancient wisdom of the church catholic knows this to be true.

That the "Earth is the Lord's" is not an affirmation that an entire culture is likely to make; but that the earth is not man's is a preliminary illumination that may open reflection to other than egocentric readings of things. In one of A. E. Housman's poems he speaks of a common human habit whereby men shut out unpleasant facts and gain a fleeting vision of the mercy of God by getting drunk. He says:

Ale, man, ale's the drink
For fellows who it hurts to think!

and adds that

Malt does more than Milton can
To justify God's ways to man!

And one may with some justice extrapolate from that that

A gasoline shortage may do more than Scripture can
To justify God's ways to man!

B. Re-opening Ways of Knowing

The second theme about which there seems to me to be a gathering solidification I shall call *a re-opening of ways of knowing and of discourse.*

That statement may seem a coldly academic and abstract way to gather up a large body of data whereby to secure the significance and power of a theological shift toward promise. But as we penetrate the meaning of the data to which I shall allude in a moment the fundamental character of that statement should be clear.

I begin that process by asking that we reflect upon that profound and subterranean demolition of assumptions, confidences, loyalties, the shattering of ideals, portraits of justice and rationality and the good life that is the fundamental fact of our culture in the past fifteen years. To assume that the causes of that demolition originated in that period would be naive; to assume that the occasions for the revolutionary actions and attitudes—the oppression of the Negro, the exposure of poverty and the callousness of public policy, the lying and deception that masked the naked brutality of the war in Vietnam—to assume that these occasions are sufficient causes would be equally naive.

Absolutely basic is a radical reduction of the meaning of the human; and it is this diminishment, in thought, in feeling, and in all forms of human engagement which is to be understood if the task of Christian theology in our time is to be undertaken, and the very possibility of Christian worship adequately proposed. To that end I point to *the contradiction of selfhood* in contemporary culture and submit that it constitutes that diminishment of the human which is the substance of the pain, longing and cry for help underneath the dramatic occasions of its utterance.

"I think, therefore I am" is an aphorism that identifies being with reflection. The fundamental error is not in the fact of thinking; men do think, and the thinking self is a function of the self. The fundamental error is rather in the naked egocentricity which is the unacknowledged postulate of the phrase. For one does not think in a self-vacuum. He does this thinking, as indeed he does whatever else he does on top of, or in the midst of, or underneath piled up accumulations and environing magnitudes.

The pathos of today's excruciating search for selfhood is not in the search. Indeed, there is adequate and commendable motivation for that. The self can stand just so much homogenization, qualification, translation into number, aggressive assault by hucksters promising to deliver the self from damnation by merging the fragile self with a million others who buy the same thing, go to the same place, or look the same way. The pathos is rather that the self accepts the invitation to become a self by actions that annul the possibility of becoming a self. For selfhood is neither a product of the accumulation of marks of individuation, nor a product of acquiescence in homogenization. The first cuts the self off; the second cuts the self down.

The self is the aware center of grateful participation. Without participation, no self; without grateful participation, a lying self. To be aware of a center presupposes a context, and to be aware of a center acknowledges that context. When St. Paul affirms that we are members one of another he does that by an organic, not organizational, analogy, the body. And this evangelical counsel builds upon an older doctrine that comes to expression in the ascription, "He hath created them in families."

When, then, I affirm that a "re-opening of ways of knowing" is a promising event in current theology, and immediately thereafter speak of the contradictions of selfhood I am suggesting that authentic cries of diminishment from contemporary selfhood are forcing a re-examination of the most prestigious model of knowledge in the modern world. That model, firmly established in empirical method and dominant in all areas of inquiry, requires an excision of the examining self from the way of knowing—and the excluded self in its anguish is the core of the spirit's protest beneath all the protestations and revolts. There is a huge analogy here. Reality, the realms of nature, history, and of human manipulation of forces based upon scientific knowledge seem indeed to constitute some kind of unity. But physics, which not so long ago aspired to become a metaphysics, has since moved from a model of unity to one of complementarity. Wave theory and particle theory of light, so long regarded as absolutely contradictory have, since R. E. Broglie, been conceived of as complementary. So also humanistic thinking has moved from older positions locked within logical principles of verification and falsification to what Heidegger calls "reflective" as against "calculative" thinking. And the fundamental postulate of reflective thinking comes out in Heidegger's claim that

> when the things of earth are approached in that
> grasping, manipulative spirit of the calculative reason
> and when our sole intent is to make them obedient to
> some enterprise of science or engineering—when they
> are simply material for one or another kind of obser-
> vation and experiment and use—then they become
> mute and fall silent. . . .it is only when we consent
> to approach it in the spirit of what Heidegger calls
> *Gelassenheit* (that is, surrender, abandonment, acqui-

escence)—it is only then that the "voice" of Being
begins to be heard. (Scott, Nathan, *The Wild Prayer
of Longing*, New Haven: Yale University Press,
1971, p. 76.)

I need not remind you of how generally that way of dealing
with *things* has, since the late nineteenth century, become also,
via the domination of scientific models in the social sciences, the
accredited way of dealing with *persons*.

It is not my task in this paper to essay pragmatic counsel. But
I must point out that the "opening" which is occurring in thought
and language carries with it promises for Christian worship. For
although whatever is primal and ultimate is "hidden and far away
because it is the source (Ursprung) of all reality, it nevertheless,
as Heidegger says, 'hails' us, and in this hailing consists precisely
the generosity with which it permits the things of earth to 'come to
presence.' Their presence, in other words, is the hail, the saluta-
tion, which Being addresses to us; and since they are present only
because Being has imparted itself to them in the manner of a
gift, any truly meditative thinking must, in effect, be an act
of thanksgiving." *(Ibid., p. 71)*.

C. Nothingness and Darkness

The third theme about which I see theological reflection solidi-
fying I shall call, borrowing the first term from Michael Novak's
book *The Experience of Nothingness, and the Fecundity of the
Darkness* (Harper and Row, 1971).

The experience of nothingness is not new. There have been
literary expressions of it in Camus, Tolstoy, Kafka—and in America as far back as Melville and Hawthorne and as recent as Saul
Bellow's *The Dangling Man*. This experience cannot be defined; it
is not a concept. But a sense for it can be descriptively built up.
Among its components are the following.

1. Contemporary consciousness is shaped by the fluidity of precepts. The film-screen and the television are fantasies of sheer

input. Things come and go like flotsam on an undifferentiated sea. Literature on the other hand is a creation; it differentiates, selects, constructs. Science, too, operates with a vigorous line of argument. But the protean shaper of the minds of millions of the young is nothing so intended, willed, controlled as these organizing efforts of older minds. The images on the screen are not sequential; their reference, in the new film, is often trans-actual. They float, things are not sequential; "time is dissolved, turned upon itself, defeated. The present gains at the expense of past and future. The attention of the camera zooms in, pulls back, superimposes—flashes back, flicks ahead. A turn of the wrist at the channel indicator alters reality, the world is fluid. The precepts are too many and too rich to order. . . ."

2. A consciousness shaped by precepts so fluid is a dispersed consciousness. Man could once declare, however erroneously, "I think, therefore I am." The dispersed consciousness cannot even begin with that assertion and order clear, distinct ideas from it as a center. In the contemporary American sub-culture the equivalent affirmation is simply "I feel." No "therefore" is available, or needed. The eye of consciousness yields to affect, percept, kaleidoscope. The self is a recipient of stimuli in a darkened room. I know I am alive when a warm body is next to mine. Connections come through skin.

3. Nothingness as boredom. For many of the young boredom has the scope and function of a kind of metaphysics. It leads to "killing time." Time, for the spirit stimulated only by fleeting fragments, is a threat. Time as duration and successiveness is the nexus within which significant action has taken place. For the bored no action is more attractive than another. Therefore time *must* be killed! The self cannot be drawn into action; it waits, upheld only by distraction from time's affirmative character. The world acts; the self is acted upon. Everything is a game.

4. Nothingness is helplessness. This feeling is far deeper than the cynicism of the young about corporate largeness, impersonality. It is not only the feeling that I have no control over my own life. It is graver than that. It is the feeling that those who wield

power are also empty, and that I, too, if I had power over my own life, am most confused about what I should do with it. The possession of power does not fill the void. The eyes of the Presidential aides disclose the same nothingness as the vacant eyes of the now silent young who but yesterday screamed at the barriers. Gone is the innocent world of that yesterday. For they, too, have found that sexuality, for instance, deprived of time-toward-something, personal intentionality that postulates a future, is sex that comes too cheaply. Its intimacy is mainly fake. They have found that even close lovers betray one another.

Recall now the second phase of this third theme—the fecundity of the darkness. Except the understanding of our task be beheld and formed in the actuality of the darkness it will be of no worth. To alter an epigram—the price exacted by the quest for the best is a steady look at the worst. And in that look let us remember and give thanks for the liberating exposures that have been accomplished: the exposure of the myth of American innocence; the exposure of the febrility of morality detached from some grave intention that is total and some trust that is transcendentally grounded; the exposure of the reality of evil and injustice behind the managed facade of growth and affluence; the exposure of the corrupting dynamics of power when power has no vision or sense of service beyond its own continuance; the exposure of idolatries garbed in the vestments of both religion and patriotism; the exposure of the hollowness of pretense, and the spirit-invigorating forms of the clean if awesome truth.

When darkness drives reflection deep it is a germinating darkness. Remember the fecundity of darkness and the night in the story of the divine redemption. In the night Jacob wrestled with the angel of his neglected God; in the night his thigh was dislocated. "So Jacob called the name of the place Peniel, saying, 'For I have seen God face to face, and yet my life is preserved.' " And then this magnificent statement—"The sun rose upon him as he passed Peniel, limping. . . ." It was upon people who walked in darkness that there came a great light. It was 'in the night in which he was betrayed' that Jesus took the cup. . . .

If, then, the fecund darkness is the strange place of light, of truth and of new life, can one discern the dynamics by which that comes about?

The experience of bewilderment amidst the crumpling of the old is a double one: on the one hand it creates anxiety about the preservation of the powers and meaning-bearing images of the very substance the old forms concentrated and transmitted. On the other hand it liberates from the necessity to behold and understand in one way only. Between these forces one is in that situation which, for all of its terror and anxiety, is the most truthful and creative man experiences. For now man must question absolutely—question all the supports offered by his culture, his faith in its received form, even the trustworthiness of his habituated consciousness. The terminus of this radical kind of questioning is potentially creative—for at the point where each comes to know that he stands alone in darkness and that he must die, he asks that fundamental human question before which both history and nature are mute. Granted that as a creature bound to and fragile in both nature and history I must die, how shall I live?

That question, without which the massive historical realities of Israel and the Christian communities cannot be accounted for, is both a sickness unto death and a supplier of the momentum in the force of which three positive, affirmative acts of the self are possible—honesty, freedom, courage.

First, *honesty*. One is forced to acknowledge that all the myths, forms, institutions by which one has lived are not necessary, solid, permanent. The first response to this knowledge is lostness. One asks, "To what purpose or end? Everything is relative. Nothing really makes any difference." But honesty does not stop with that. For in honesty one knows that relativity is not an absolute. "It is simply a fact. Just as we discovered, through the drive to question, that values are relative, so now we discover, through the same drive, the relativity of relativity! The fact that values are relative to one's culture, time, person and purpose does not oblige us to be ethically indifferent: a mere fact is not normative. Relativity describes a state of affairs. It is not an excuse but a starting point. Granted that values are relative, how do I wish to live? The ethical question becomes a question of invention and creativity rather than a problem of obedience and obligation." (Michael Novak, *The Experience of Nothingness*, p. 52f.). This movement beyond relativity is not theory but fact. I know no man of intelligence who does not experience relativity; I know no man who lives and acts as if relativity were an absolute.

That fact, that we do act, that out of theoretical darkness we choose, is the reality of *freedom*. And in that act of freedom we make a huge leap—for we thereby confer a value upon the drive to question and fact of choice. Nothing compels us to turn facts into values. To do this is an act of freedom, a creative act whose starting-place is in the very fecundity of darkness. It is in very truth a *creatio ex nihilo*.

If anyone should suppose that in this quite interior analysis of how darkness moves toward light I am ignoring the fundamental Christian theological affirmations of the faith, he is confusing the absence of conventional rhetoric for an absence of Christian substance. For there is a sense, sharper and more profound as one matures in the faith, in which he comes to know that the spirit that hovered over chaos, darkness and old ancient might in the creation, operates with equivalent cruciality in the realm and reality of redemption. The Christian prayer *Veni Creator Spiritus* postulates, to be sure, an incarnated presence in Jesus Christ which has a clarity that surpasses the spirit as known by the First Adam; but the act of choice-out-of-darkness by which the Second Adam was declared Son of God in power was an act of faith—and requires a recapitulated act of faith from every baptized child of that Second Adam, the pioneer and finisher of the New Creation.

So, then, the third act, experienced in and out of the fecund darkness, is *courage*. Without courage honesty is impossible; one avoids truth. Without courage, freedom is impossible; one lacks the heart to create. The Spirit *is* honesty, the Spirit *is* freedom, and the Spirit *is* courage. When our fathers confessed the Spirit to be "the Lord and Giver of Life" they did not by that confession annul the prophetic and apostolic injunction that "the Spirit bears witness *with* our spirit" that we are to "be of good courage."

Summary Propositions

And now, in a brief final section I shall try to extrapolate from the foregoing what I think to be fruitful propositions for this week's discussion.

1. *Dogma and doxa,* what we believe and what we pray, constitute a single music in contrapuntal form. The somber remembrances and the fresh probings of the faith as *doxa* always illuminate and freshly unfold the intelligibility and power of the faith as *dogma.* The songs of praise the church sings are a lyrical way of disclosing what the faith knows—and *how* she knows. The language of recollection, thanksgiving and joy—which is praise, is at the same time the alembic in which a new conceptuality, and a language serviceable to be its voice is freshly forged.

2. The issues that have called us together must be attacked and struggled with by the church, within the church, for the church. That statement is so flat, to some perhaps so reductive and even contrary to guiding assumptions in contemporary liturgical thought that I ask leave to expand it.

Faith, community, worship and work—these are not separate items in any truly catholic understanding of the church; they are rather the energies of its organic reality. That means that worship *is* a cultic ritual—but in a double sense Christian worship *is* a ritual of a cult in the sense that the terms it uses, the recollections it cherishes, the episodes it orders toward significance, the images and symbols it employs are drenched in the shared meanings of a very particular community. Dogma bears forth doxa; and doxa both explores and enriches dogma.

But there is an equally important sense in which Christian worship is *not* the ritual of a cult. Its action is a public action; it speaks within the culture always wanting to be overheard. Its affirmations are not founded upon the culture, but they are an address, through the community, to the culture. The world does not know why the church says what it says; but what the church says is not esoteric or unintelligible. The life of the cult forms what is to be said; but the promises recalled, the powers and presences celebrated, the mad hopes that swing out from and resonate beyond the cult—these strangely intersect with the inarticulated realities of the world-around.

This double-character of Christian worship says something, too, about the form, style, language of worship. The impact of the reality of the faith, as that comes to expression in worship, has always been and I think will continue to be most effective beyond the cult when the making of an impact is not a primary intention. That impact is most productive, its force most free when its own order, content and passion is true to its interior substances. The church best serves the culture by not intending primarily to serve the culture; she discloses best what the culture needs when she speaks out of her own integrity. To be "with it" may actually come about by no intention to be "with it." For culture has the strange habit of translating powers and forces not its own into fresh questions about itself.

There is, to be sure, a shaping interaction between Christ and culture. The modes of a culture are not without influence upon the form and language of worship. That interplay of influences, however, is most integrally absorbed and actualized by both when imitation is not employed, trading-off gimmicks not allowed. The deepest influence takes place without such intention and is the better for it. The authorized version of the Scripture did not intend to ape the opulence of Elizabethan English; the rhetorical miracle was achieved because a gravity of intention became invested with a garment that matched its magnificence. The symbiotic language-event that operated in our language between Chaucer and Milton —with Shakespeare in between—required no managed intentions.

The purpose of this opening paper has been suggestive, not programmatic. It has tried only to open and expound what I believe to be theological facts for our time, and urge that darkness, eschatologically understood, has a strange truth-bearing power.

Henry E. Horn

Worship:
The Gospel in Action

If this Conference on Worship had been held thirty years ago, a mere parish pastor would not have dared to grace this platform. In those days we all looked to *the authorities* on such subjects; and there were only two directions one would look for the last word on worship. The obvious first was to the liturgical scholars, the Luther D. Reeds, and the Paul Zeller Strodachs, whose monumental knowledge of what was done when and what should be done now was held in awe by all of us; the other was over the shoulder a bit to the theologians whose critical eyes could isolate the "unLutheran" virus in the midst of our worship. It was obvious that the two had not come together; the cannonading went on over our heads between the two camps. So the parish pastor was always damned if he did, and damned if he didn't.

That was thirty years ago. A lot has happened in worship in the years of my ministry. The modern, post Vatican II liturgical movement has brought about great changes: one now talks of worship as action; worship belongs to the whole people of God; leadership is spread among the people; the language and idiom of the people—"folk"—is the thing; the whole human sensorium is now involved in celebration; human festivity and a theology of play dominate the moods expected.[1]

24

Leadership in Worship Today

Ambiguity still pervades the parsonage, however. For many parish pastors, the change is gloriously welcome. Rigid control of the liturgy by church convention action or by strict rubrical regulation has been broken. Scratching a Dionysian itch is now no longer a matter of the exclusively private domain. The whole world of expressive and subjective worship, just laid to rest in many parishes, can be brought forth again, if only the Hallelujah hymnals can be located in the tower room. The movement has its built-in self justification. If one can just effect the actions of the people, according to some reasonable shape; if these people know what they are doing; then there is assumed to be a built-in satisfaction of some kind. *The authorities*—both of them—be hanged!

Other pastors, not quite freed from the haunting feeling that there is some authority remaining in the church, look back over their shoulders for direction from somebody. But there aren't any Reeds in sight. Even at the seminaries one can't find guidance. The layman would assume that the focal point of his own relationship with the church—the regular worship of the congregation—would be the starting point for ministerial training. My own experience on the Board of Theological Education leads me to whisper that worship and the life of prayer is the most embarrassing area of seminary education today.[2]

I have found the systematic theologians most concerned about the current rush toward "celebration." Their aim of opening up the true gospel at every possible meeting of the congregation brings them into deep concern for the worship of the church. They see a superficial display of feeling and self-expression covering up the prophetic Word, the way of the cross, the pain which precedes resurrection, and the eschatological character of faith, hope and love. To them, renewal without conversion through the gospel, is self-delusion.[3]

But a good deal of the language of our theologians is in terms of a past when one approached reality through rational discourse, and then applied ideas of generalized truth to particular situations. In many ways the terms *law* and *gospel,* so dear to Lutherans, come to us through this approach. And even though we recognize their truth as ideas, our modern emphasis is to experience reality fully with unobstructed feeling. Encounter groups, transactional analysis experience, almost any foray into feeling is of much more essential value to persons as a way to truth today. So we are in no real position to stop and think right now, for there are new experiences to savor.

So neither liturgical specialists nor theologians serve as authority for us any more. Where has the spotlight shifted? Where shall we discover new authority for our leadership in worship? Where shall we discover the essential integrity of our actions?

We could guess by listening to the changes in our styles of life today. Certainly we have seen the spotlight move away from generalizations to specifics, from conceptual approaches to truth to individual events and happenings, from objective-centered approaches to management to discovering the appearance of surprises in daily events. If the youth revolution has taught us nothing else, it has turned the spotlight upon individual happenings, the depth and breadth of experience at individual events of life. The fact that "there is much more than meets the eye" in life's events is certainly responsible for the movement toward Eastern meditation, encounter group experience, transactional analysis, the use of consciousness expanding drugs, etc. This massive shift of attention has wrenched the spotlight away from the specialists such as theologians to center on individual events, isolated happenings which provide the real stuff of new life. In short, attention is now centered upon the event of public worship every time it happens.

When one examines the planning and budgeting of the church during the years of my ministry, these processes have seemed to be blind to this recent development. Management theory has been borrowed from large operations;[4] planning-by-objectives has dominated the working day of church leaders—as if we could easily plan our future in a church which lives by its meetings with reality, and by the process of conversion-through-meeting. If, as we claim, anything real happens in the meeting between our Father and his people, through the mediation of Jesus Christ, then this must affect our whole being. The church's task in worship is to provide the setting for this happening in depth. This should demand the concentrated attention of the whole church again and ever again.

Certainly there are few pastors who at *some* time in their ministry have not been overawed at the responsibility of their leadership in worship. If we have not imagined the dynamics of this meeting, we have surely seen what absence from worship does to the living faith of members, and what a difference return to worship makes in the same persons. Even if one is not open to the reverberations and vibrations in the event itself, there is a normative function performed in the event which makes the act the guardian of the integrity of the Christian life.[5] We know well that the real life of the church is found here; not in our statistics or our project descriptions. It is out of the event of worship that new authority can come to the faith and life of the church. Leaders of worship are midwives of that authority. This is the general theme that I now wish to pursue.

The Importance of the Theologian

Perhaps the most important ally of the pastor as leader in worship is the theologian today, as I have suggested. But the shifting of the spotlight to the event of worship requires a like turning of our ideas of the relationship of the theologian and the preacher. Paul Ricoeur, the French Protestant philosopher, has provided a new orientation in an essay entitled prophetically in this day of Watergate, *Truth and Falsehood.*[6] He starts with the Christian confession that when we approach truth, we approach the person of Jesus Christ. That is, for the Christian, truth at its heart is the person. Therefore the apprehension of truth does not come merely from the acceptance of intellectual material; it comes in an encounter between persons, a meeting in which the dialogue, spoken or unspoken, changes each. No one can predict what will happen after such a meeting. Certainly the person seeking truth is never the same thereafter. There are reverberations and resonations to the very depth of his being. One leaves the meeting having been "converted," changed by the encounter. You will recognize in this description all of the dynamics of post-Buberian thinking which opened to us a whole theology of encounter and Word-event.

Now, Ricoeur says, to bring us to a meeting with the truth which is Person we need testimonies, witnesses, "the finger which points. The first testimony is Scripture. Through the forms and acts of worship, preaching transmits and explains to the community of today the primary testimony (Scripture). Thus if there is a truth to preaching it must lie in its conformity to the testimony concerning the Truth-Person. . . . But as preaching is always an act which takes place in the present, it already introduces the dialectical characters of human truth; it too dialecticizes itself between the two mortal poles of anachronistic repetition and hazardous adaptation of the Word to the present need of the community of the faithful. The truth of preaching is therefore always in search of a fidelity which would be creative." [7]

Preaching, for Ricoeur, the reformed Protestant, stands for worship for the Lutheran, and I shall later maintain that they are slightly different. But Ricoeur then goes on to say that theology is really one step removed from this preaching in worship. Theology does not have direct access to the truth. Instead it is the episodic attempt of the preacher to effect a real meeting between the truth and the believers time after time that constitutes the material for theology. Theology is reflection upon the faith and life of the church. The theologian has several tasks to perform with respect to this material. 1) He judges preaching and worship to see that it measures against the Word of God— that is—that it points faithfully to the testimony; 2) he makes into one whole the scattered episodes of preaching and worship —trying to form some reasonable model of the totality; 3) he has to carry on a constant dialogue with the culture of his day from the truth that he knows.

The point that Ricoeur makes is clear. He shifts the meeting place between the believer and truth to those events which happen in the context of worship and prayer. Suddenly one begins to be sensitive to the hum of generators of new life in the acts of worship. We who lead in worship have always had a faint suspicion that this was so. Except for the verbal gestures in this direction, it has been difficult to find any confirmation of this emphasis in the practice of the whole church, or in the traditional theologies. How often has the preacher tried desperately to present the truth after careful exegesis and daring application one Sunday only to find himself, by use of the same rigorous honesty the next Sunday saying almost the opposite thing in another episode of meeting. Faithfulness to the truth as he meets it has led him to inconsistency—and such as is characteristic of living persons. But we are thankful that the theologians must wrestle with these problems and provide the test of faithfulness as well as the model of some consistency. Ricoeur would simply emphasize the primary nature of the data gained from meeting in different times and places of life as the fountainhead of the church's life and faith.

Preaching, as I suggested, from the testimony of the Scriptures is to Ricoeur the fountainhead itself. Lutherans can applaud this emphasis. Lutheran theologians would probably say, Amen. But my whole experience in Lutheran worship and my reading of early Lutheran writers convinces me that there is much more to the encounter with the Word in a believing congregation than testimony via the preached word. Elsewhere I have referred to a very significant address given by Prof. Heikko Oberman, then of Harvard, to help reclaim Protestant preaching today.[8] He showed how the great Reformers, Luther, Calvin, Zwingli, believed in a sacramental conception of the Word of God. Though they denied the automatic effect of the sacrament of Holy Communion, they actually transferred this effect to the preaching of the Word. Thus they always spoke of Christ being actually present whenever the word is preached, effecting his work. The belief in *ex opere operato* in the administration of the Holy Communion was transferred by the Reformers into the preaching of the Word. Oberman then told of the disappearance of this concept of presence and built-in effect from Protestant preaching, and the consequent remainder in the form of a disembodied intellectual message. The result is evident in the abstract character of Protestant worship today.

Wilhelm Stählin has characterized Lutherans as those who doggedly held on to a Real Presence in the Holy Communion even while they made unsuccessful attempts at providing any definition of what they meant.[9] Their ineffective arguments always broke down, yet they would still point to the fact that "there is much more there than meets the eye." My students tell me I am terribly naive to believe in this presence in worship, and in the continued effectiveness of the preached word. Yet for me the whole context is that of greeting a Person, the Truth, enfleshed in a series of episodes which are then opened up for meeting. That Person comes to us in episodes of events retold and relived. Through meetings with him we are led to the Father and made into his people.[10]

Of course, words are important, but a purely verbal exercise is not enough. If the testimony points to the Person, and we believe in the re-presentation of that Person, than some sense of this presence, imagined or real, must pervade our consciousness and have its resonations in our movements and actions. The dramatic actions of entrance into this presence must be clearly felt. In my attempts to provide for this happening, my overriding question in preparation for worship has been, "How does our Lord come to us through the lessons of the day? How does he lead us to the Father? What does the Father require of us as a people now?"

The Need of a Prophetic Faith

It is quite evident that such a position brings disbelief from some theologians. In their eyes I have just brought in some mystical mumbo-jumbo into Lutheran worship which a direct confrontation with the Word of God—law and gospel would expose. The famous polarization of Rudolph Otto of a) prophetic religion, and b) mystical religion, is invoked, and I am suddenly exposed in my mysticism. This implies the absence of the prophetic faith which is nurtured by the proclamation of the Word of God: law and gospel.[11]

Now certainly all of us are somewhat lacking in the prophetic faith in these prophetic times. Though it should be pointed out that the modern liturgical movement, setting the people of God's celebration squarely in the midst of their very own world, has transformed a number of Christians into social activists and brought forth a theology of liberation, it is by no means automatic that such renewal of congregational worship will transform middle class worshipers into prophetic figures. Many have hopefully instituted changes, and have been keenly disappointed at the mystical aestheticism that takes over, moving constantly in a swirling and decreasing group of the avant garde. Unless the prophetic Word is present, our worship lacks the content which brings the conversion meeting. The real Lord is not there.

On the other hand, our traditional theology, while paying lip service to the Real Presence, shows no sign of dynamism that this presence brings. Dietrich Ritschl has pointed this out in a significant book, *Memory and Hope*.[12] Ritschl, writing concurrently with Jurgen Moltmann, maintains that a theology of hope is what is needed today. We need to reach into future promises and celebrate them as present even if this distorts our own present. But he, as distinct from Moltmann, provides the center for the celebration—the Person. Forgotten by the theologian—and often by the liturgist—is the reality of *Christus praesens* (Christ making himself present) throughout the history of the church. According to Ritschl, the concept of *Christus praesens,* so obviously present from the time of the post-resurrection appearances, was forgotten when a static concept of God as Perfection took over the West. God was removed from the flow of time and space. The world was not thought of as the place of his presence. Instead another realm was developed in thought. The Risen Christ then becomes a bit of history that inspires our faith and becomes effective to the degree that faith is nourished by that backward glance to The Event. The Lord-to-come is even raised above us as Perfection. The ideal of life then becomes to see the beatific vision (heaven) and sainthood is the state where this becomes reality. Blood, sweat, and tears—the sign of sainthood today—was hardly the setting for the beatific vision.

For Ritschl, the missing and all important dynamic is *Christus praesens,* always hidden and therefore giving life to Christian worship, not simply a principle in Christian experience. He attempts to restore *Christus praesens* to the center of theological reflection; theology then becomes reflection upon the life of the people of God gathered around this Christ-on-the-way-to-becoming-Lord; reflection upon the process by which that which is hoped for comes to be. In so doing, he gives theological argument for that which I have been seeking—as a pastor—in weekly worship. It is this *Christus praesens* under forms of proclamation and celebration—"where two or three are gathered in my name, there am I in the midst of them"—that enlivens our faith and inspires our hope. This presence, always confessed by Lutherans but rarely imagined, *is* imagined in a celebrative mood.

My use of the suggestion of imagination may cause some apostles of the Word to lift their eyebrows a bit. Our traditionally conceptual approach to the gospel makes us susceptible to total definition of everything. But the new theology of hope has provided grounds for reorientation. It suggests that the pathway to faith today is not through the acceptance of conceptual beliefs, but by the indirect path of a celebration of those things that we can hope for. And through our hope, we are pulled into fulfilled promises which move toward us from the gracious Father. One is drawn into a dynamic process in which he moves "from faith to faith." The presence of Christ in worship is that dramatic reality that stimulates our imagination, enlivens our hope, and pushes us toward the promises. In this process we are drawn into the reality of the coming kingdom; we live as though it were realized. We are eschatological persons.

It is not surprising to me that some sense of presence is the key to Christian worship. The recent movements which have recovered the basic shapes of the proclamation of the Word and the celebration around the table in a believing congregation demonstrate actions which assume a Presence. Louis Bouyer in *Liturgical Piety* shows the development of the "preaching service" from the shape of the meeting of the gathered community with its God in the Old Testament.[13] Without this shape the whole action doesn't make much sense. Who would ever gather with preparations to listen to the readings from so-called sacred authors, centuries out of date, unless they pointed to a possible living Presence? Gregory Dix has shown the development of the Eucharist around the imitative actions of our Lord in the meal.[14] What real meaning can this shape, this meal, have except as it pulls one into a new reality, not yet fully consummated?

It is right that the theologian should have his tongue in his cheek as he tries to make reasonable sense of these signs of the church's faith and life. One would hope that he would be rigorous in checking the purity of the testimony, to see that it is truly the Lord that is pointed to. He should be fearless in his application of the normative correction of the testimony. He should also try to show us what we have discovered in some model as well as help us to talk of our faith in today's world. But he should not limit the depth and breadth of our experience in meeting by some theoretical assumption that it cannot be so. This is a day when surprises are expected in life. The social scientist who yesterday wrote off religious phenomena because of his acceptance of generalized assumptions which left no place for religion, now accepts as proper data the individual events of man's life in all their richness. To put together such phenomena— episodes of meeting—in the construct of a new science is, of course, the "in thing." Phenomenology of religion is the promising approach for any young man who wants to enter the teaching of the subject.[15]

A New Kind of Conversion

It is not that theologians are unaware of the importance of a new start in the dynamics of encounter.[16] They were talking in the 40s and 50s of the dynamic aspects of the Word of God as event, and the proclamation of the Word as actually moving into a man and taking hold of his whole being—pulling him inside out in conversion. But too often among Lutherans, there seemed to be a great gap between the liturgical specialists and the theologians; they did not approach the problem of worship together. Instead the center of worship remained preaching for many of the theologians of the Word.

However, we are seeing an amazing confluence of various currents in the Roman Catholic Church now. Nourished in a theology of the Word as event, we find scholars who naturally apply this to the whole event of worship and out of it comes affirmations that confirm my own experience. The language is not familiar Lutheran language. Kerygma—or proclamation of the New Testament gospel—replaces terms like law and gospel. The signs of the coming kingdom now present—exorcism of demons, forgiveness of sins, the power of the Spirit—suddenly replace the old language. But at the heart of the meeting is the renewal of man and the turning of his actions toward those of the kingdom.[17] Bernard Lonergan has described this process of change:

> Fundamental to all religious living is conversion
> . . . it is not merely a change, or even a development;
> rather it is a radical transformation on which fol-
> lows, on all levels of living, an interlocked series of
> changes and developments. What hitherto was un-
> noticed becomes vivid and present. So great a change
> in one's apprehensions and one's values accompanies
> no less a change in oneself, in one's relations to
> God. . . .
> When conversion is viewed as an ongoing process
> at once personal, communal and historical, it coin-
> cides with living religion. For religion is conversion
> in its preparation, in its occurrence, in its conse-
> quents, and also alas, in its incompleteness, its failure,
> its breakdowns, its disintegration. . . .[18]

That almost sounds like a rally cry for Evangelism Key 73. But for some of us that is where the similarity stops. Our whole concept of conversion has been entirely too shallow. "Incompleteness, failure, breakdown, disintegration" are indeed characteristic of our popular movements. They hold our Lord closely entwined with middle-class ethics. Why should those who mouth the clichés the loudest exhibit the most conservative way of life? This is a problem that a generation of youth has had to grapple with. The youth are the inheritors of "incompleteness, failure, breakdown, disintegration" of the conversion process of their elders.

This massive failure of Christian conversion is now exposed.

Those of us in university centers have seen one wave of attack after another on the accepted Christian way of life: first the Freedom Movement, then the Black Consciousness Movement; then the Third World Revolution; then the Student Revolt; then the Peace Movement. That things are quiet now is no grounds for just wiping out a decade of earnest protest from our memories. For the protest was often against the very ground on which many of us take our stand. I do not wish to irritate everyone by dwelling in negatives except to say that today, the liveliest theological movement arises out of Latin America from the experience of the oppressed. It is called the theology of liberation, and a portion of it is called hopefully, *A Theology for Artisans of a New Humanity.*[19] It is sufficient to say that a theology of the oppressed contains many negatives for a theology of the oppressor.

Three Aspects of Modern Consciousness

Of course, we feel the negatives. We hardly feel the vibrations of positive discoveries in our day. These positive discoveries of human experience pervade the consciousness of our youth. One who serves in the university in this decade cannot ignore them; for they constitute the life-space within which the gospel must come into action. I have selected three aspects of this modern consciousness.[20]

1) There is a new search for depth experiences which involve one's whole self. The day of superficial conformity to someone else's experience is over. One cannot count on any code of ethics to control, nor accepted manners to direct the experience of the younger generation. This is the time when everyone knows that life is deeper than meets the eye; there are experiences of depth and breadth awaiting everyone, and a short time in which to live; there are reverberations and vibrations of every experience which lie undiscovered by most of us.

A type of worship which is cut and dried, be it a liturgy perfectly "done," or an intellectual presentation convincingly argued, is too neat for life's depths today. The spirit of wonder and awe

at the ordinary things of life, the ordinary "happenings" has been
stumbled on by many young people in search of their primitive
creaturehood. Fortunately for those interested in Christian worship, we too have been led to a rediscovery of much the same
thing in our tradition, largely by the discoveries of biblical theology and the language of Scripture. For there is a remarkable
similarity between the poetic language of Scripture, its sense of
presence, its concept of the Word as word-event and the new
awareness of depth in human experience. Indeed, the whole concept of "praise" is really a depth phenomenon. In the act of praise,
the worshiper is grabbed at the bottom of his life and pulled
inside out in response to the majestic goodness of God; movement, singing—all those actions which involve the whole being
move in concert toward the Father. Therefore, I can only see that
the act of worship, the meeting of man with God in worship,
is precisely tailor-made for modern man. Where all of the arts
are used creatively in acts of worship, where the presence is assumed and felt, the younger generation can be met with joy—
provided their former disappointments have not turned them off
forever.

2) There is a hunger for deep human interrelationships. How
else can we explain the spread of "T groups," support groups,
encounter groups, communal living, transactional analysis? For
a decade now, young people who hear that the congregation is a
"community" have demanded that it show these signs in actuality;
and having studied community in depth, they are really disappointed to find the word community loosely used. Some sociologists have claimed that there is a great drive for intimacy today
—just that intimacy which formerly was reserved for a life mate.
Many recognize no justification for one to play any roles to
protect his essential being. This means that for many one cannot
maintain the distinction between the public and the private life,
between corporate worship and private prayer.

In experiments with new modes of worship, some of us have
been embarrassed by this drive for intimacy. Interrelatedness of
feeling is attempted; emotional expression is encouraged; the

liturgical kiss of peace is actualized in hugs and kisses; it seems to be just assumed that immediate intimacy is the result of genuine worship.

As I have attempted to argue elsewhere,[21] this poses a serious dilemma for those who care for public worship. Personally, I believe that role playing and public language actually protects the essential self just so that it can speak forth with more freedom and certainty; therefore, I would maintain that the distinction between corporate and private methods of expression must be maintained—even in the interests of human freedom. But certainly a new type of radical honesty is needed in both spheres if we are to minister to this generation. And honesty and integrity in the public sphere of our life today is the great challenge to the church.

3) There is a new solidarity felt by the sensitive for the totality of humanity on this planet. How else can one explain the revolutions of the sixties? The expectation that when one suffers, all suffer seems to be built into the modern consciousness of one world. The grief our sons and daughters felt for the people of Viet Nam was embarrassingly real, as any campus pastor can testify.

My own generation cannot understand this except by conversion. Conversion to this viewpoint comes through regular steps that have to be taken one by one. It goes something like this: first, we feel sorry for the oppressed and seek to help them in our own way; then suddenly we are confronted by them as they angrily tell us that they themselves want to determine the content of their needs—our own assessments according to our own judgment are in error; but they haven't the freedom to imagine their own needs; then we see that it is *our freedom* that is their slavery.[22] Unless we do something about this primary, and of course obvious, fact, there is really no conversion at all.

From the aspect of human solidarity, our great campaign of evangelism appear to be exercises in futility. We still remain unconverted. We still plough along in our accepted way of life. For true conversion for most of us in these years has come from the area of our social life. We have been sharply challenged and surely turned by our contacts with the oppressed. Though we do not like the charge of being racist, sexist, imperialist, colonialist, we now can see that the ending "ist" applied to us usually stands for one who is unconverted.

Here the theologian can help us. The plight of the poor has brought insights into the reality of Christ as Liberator. Suddenly the theologian can guide the preacher to the testimony which reveals the true Lord. The pastor, leading worship, can provide the meeting place where this Truth can engage the people. And in episode after episode, the conversion of the people of God can take place.

These three aspects of modern consciousness—the new search for depth experiences, the hunger for deep interrelationships, the new sense of human solidarity—determine the weather currents among the people I know and serve. In the past decade I have seen many a colleague swept away in the fads that these currents generate. For instance, all sorts of experiments have taken place to intensify human experience, from drug intensified sexual experience to Zen and Eastern meditation; group experiences have, in many congregations, been equated with Christian worship; gratification of the feeling of human solidarity has taken the place of worship for many who have just left the church in disgust.

This seems to me to have been a great waste. For within the act of worship-come-alive there are the depths which are being sought. Moreover, at the center of this act is the glorious Good News of God's grace and presence to his people, the first taste of that which is to come. In celebration of this hoped-for-reality, we are drawn into the whole world of his action among his people.

We desperately need the theologian to see that the proper testimonies and witnesses are used in worship—this act must be normative for the Christian life. We expect them to watch over the context of our faith and life and put together all of our experience in faith. Specialists are not out of date if their specialty serves the purpose of this revelation that we seek. In the absence of any real movement of the church toward the renewal of its worship, we call upon pastors and theologians to do their particular duty with expectant devotion.

This *is* a changed day. The spotlight of hope is focused on our weekly worship. If there is to be new life in the church, we can expect it to rise out of the fountainhead of the church's worship. The shape of that renewal is not clear. It cannot be written two years in advance in project descriptions by futurists. It cannot even be prepared for in pre-planned sermons, or in projected experimentation in worship. It will happen when leaders of worship, faithful to the testimony, and expectant of the presence, are willing to celebrate the signs of the kingdom now at work in our world.

Notes

1. I have tried to describe this in *Worship in Crisis* (Fortress Press, Philadelphia, 1972).
2. Present embarrassment for available funding has dried up sources for providing professors in worship. It is a rare seminarian who enters his first parish prepared for the leadership of worship.
3. See especially the article, "Orpheus the Button-maker and Real Community" by Robert Jenson in *Dialog* (Volume 10, Winter 1971).
4. I refer here directly to the transformation of church planning to PPB Systems. On the local level congregations will have to justify objectives for funding.
5. Recently I was present at the celebration in behalf of a Christian community worker where he was found to be a man of integrity and compassion. It was easy to see that this discipline was the result of the normative function of his weekly worship.
6. See p. 165 ff. of *History and Truth* by Paul Ricoeur, edited by Charles A. Kelbley (Northwestern University Press, Evanston, 1965).
7. See same, p. 177.
8. See Heikko A. Oberman, "The Preaching of the Word," *Harvard Divinity School Bulletin* (October, 1960), pp. 7-18, especially the following: "I should like to suggest that the genius of the Reformation is best described as the rediscovery of the Holy Spirit, the present Christ. . . ."
9. See Wilhelm Stählin, *The Mystery of God* (Concordia Publishing House, St. Louis, 1964).
10. I have described my position in *Lutherans in Campus Ministry*, pp. 148 ff; (National Lutheran Council Ministry, Chicago, 1969).
11. This criticism has actually come to me through letters in response to my *Worship in Crisis*.
12. See Dietrich Ritschl, *Memory and Hope* (Macmillan, New York, 1967).
13. See Louis Bouyer, *Liturgical Piety* (Notre Dame University Press, Notre Dame, Ind., 1955).

14. See Gregory Dix, *The Shape of the Liturgy* (Alec R. Alleson, Inc., Naperville, Ill. 1964).

15. Whereas in past years liturgical specialists were developed out of historians, today we should expect them to arise out of anthropolgists, sociologists, psychologists—those who deal with the phenomena of man's social life.

16. See especially the work of the post-Bultmannians such as Fuchs, Ebeling, etc.

17. See Gerard Lukkem in "The Unique Expression of Faith in the Liturgy" pp. 11-21 in *Liturgical Experience of Faith,* edited by Herman Schmidt and David Power in Concilium II (Herder and Herder, New York, 1973).

18. See Bernard Lonergan, pp. 44, 45 in "Theology in Its New Context" in *Theology of Renewal* edited by L. K. Shook, C.S.B. (Herder and Herder, New York, 1968, Vol. I).

19. See Juan Luis Segundo, S. J., *The Community Called Church* and *Grace and the Human Condition* (Orbis Books, Maryknoll, N.Y., 1973), Volumes I and II.

20. Some of the shape of this section has been influenced by a volume edited by Andrew Greeley and Gregory Baum in Concilium II, *The Persistence of Religion.* See especially the article by Greeley, "The Persistence of Community" for what follows. His remarks simply have provided some organization for my rich experience in these past years.

21. See *Worship in Crisis,* Chapters 4 and 5.

22. I am indebted to John Harmon of Packard Manse for an early journey along this route. My experience in working with the dispossessed makes me feel that all of us have to travel this route to find human reality in our time. One doesn't need to be accused of being Marxist to feel this way; it follows from one's belief in the liberating character of the gospel itself.

James F. White

Worship
in Our Changing Culture

In the *Constitution on the Sacred Liturgy* of Vatican II there is an intriguing statement: "For the liturgy is made up of immutable elements divinely instituted, and of elements subject to change." [1] It goes on to say that the latter "not only may but ought to be changed with the passage of time if they have suffered from the intrusion of anything out of harmony with the inner nature of the liturgy or have become unsuited to it." Unfortunately for us, the fathers of Vatican II did not specify which were the unchangeable elements and which were those subject to change. What they hesitated to do, I shall try to sort out in this brief essay. This may seem bold, but it seems to me that we have before us the number one problem in Christian worship today, that is, trying to sort out the changing cultural contexts of Christian worship from the changeless norms of such worship. First we shall investigate the changing cultural contexts of Protestant worship in America during the past hundred years. Then we shall try to define the changeless norms in worship which have remained constant despite the changing cultural contexts.

A Century of Change

During the past hundred years, the forms of Protestant worship in America have reflected four quite different cultural epochs. We may be inclined to fault Catholic worship because it has had only one cultural shift in that period, the thaw after Vatican II. But some would feel that the worship of the central churches in American Protestantism—Methodists, Congregationalists, Presbyterians, and Disciples—mirrored too closely the changing cultural patterns of this century. Lutherans, Episcopalians, and a few German Reformed managed to avoid some of these currents or even to react against them. But even in so doing they were often reflecting counter-cultural patterns based on ethnic origins or romanticism.

For the first half of the past century, the period from 1870 to 1920, the dominant pattern in worship in central Protestantism showed the strong impact of revivalism. Worship tended to become a means to an end, the making of converts and the nourishing of those already converted. With such a purpose in mind, it became possible to shape worship to a practical and purposeful end, i.e., it worked. Whatever criticisms we may have of the effects of nineteenth-century revivalism upon worship, we cannot overlook the pragmatic character of it. A century earlier, Jonathan Edwards had written his *Faithful Narrative of the Surprising Work of God* (1737). Almost exactly a hundred years later appeared Charles G. Finney's *Lectures on Revivals of Religion* (1835). Edwards chronicles with amazement; Finney's book is a how-to-do manual with the results almost guaranteed if one follows the proper techniques. Plant the proper grain and the wheat will appear.

Finney's book could well stand as the prime example of this period in worship. Bold, brusk, and vigorous, he traces changes in worship only to show that nothing has abided long and therefore the preacher is free to ignore history and to introduce "new measures" that will be effective. Behind all this is the pragmatic optimism of the time. America had been liberated from the dead hand of the past and the future was dazzling. Call it manifest destiny, the age of reform, the frontier spirit, Horatio Alger, it had one thrust—use the right techniques and there was no limit to what could be accomplished.

Let us not be negative about the degree to which it worked. It christianized a nation whose founding fathers had hardly been godly, righteous, or sober, despite myths to the contrary. And it gave vigor to dozens of reform movements including abolition. But it did have its faults, though today, after reacting against revivalism for half a century, we can see some of its virtues as well.

Its chief fault was that theologically it was weak. Dividing humanity into the saved and the lost does simplify things considerably. But there are contradictions in the phrase: "bringing souls to Christ." And trying to snatch them from outer darkness into the bright radiance of salvation by an instantaneous occurrence caused problems. It was easy to neglect children until they were ripe for conversion and the passion for recruiting the outsider tended to overwhelm the care and discipline of those within the fold. The traditional means of grace were too easily replaced by more sensational new measures.

But theologically weak as it was, revivalism had some elements of keen psychological insight that we have had to relearn in the last five years. For one thing, revivalism knew that in order to move people spiritually you have to move them physically. We have seen a spate of books recently such as *The Body at Liturgy*,[2] etc. The church music which we told people for years was not good for them (and they still requested) was based on the realization that music is a body art. Even more important was the element of spontaneity, the unexpected possibility in worship. When the 1905 *Methodist Hymnal* included an "Order of Worship" there was an outcry against such unfamiliar formality. Is it any wonder that older people in our churches have a curious nostalgia after the worship of this period no matter how hard seminary-trained clergy discourage such hankering after the flesh-pots of Egypt? Revivalism may have been theologically weak but it understood people and did a fine job of reflecting many of the dominant currents of nineteenth-century American culture.

But cultural currents were changing and the 1920s saw a new era emerging in worship too. I would call this the era of respectability and would divide it into two periods: one a period of aestheticism and the other a period of historicism. The era of respectability in Protestant worship was the half century beginning in the early 1920s. It represents the assertion of sobriety over the ecstatic, of refinement over the primitive, of restraint over the boisterous. It was a reflection of the increased sophistication of Americans as education became available to most. There was a neat correlation between the changes in the educational level of the average Methodist and what was happening to his worship life. The displays of emotion, the freedom and spontaneity, the general folksiness of revivalism were all pushed aside or left behind for those who had not yet ascended the social and educational scale.

The first half of our period of respectability, roughly 1920 to 1945, saw a substitution for worship as a conversion experience (or renewal of such an experience) of worship as an aesthetic experience. The slogan, despite its inherent contradiction, was: "enriching our worship." America is dotted with churches, usually gothic where the budget would allow, that reflect both the wealth and sophistication of the period. These are examples of the second gothic revival, not the robust and original gothic of the 1840s and 1850s but the academically correct gothic of the 1920s. The buildings contain accurate copies of medieval elements, correct, timid, and in good taste. For good taste had invaded the sanctuary and replaced the pragmatic, functional, though hopelessly unsophisticated Akron plan. Good taste had invaded the choir loft and replaced the folksy quartet or octet with a full-fledged choir singing "good" music by composers all a century safely dead. Good taste had created a formal order of worship so that Methodists, by 1932, had several orders of worship to choose from and by 1944 a whole *Book of Worship*. And the greatest liturgical innovator since Gutenberg, a Mr. A. B. Dick, had given each minister a printing press in the form of a mimeograph. Now no one had to worry about saying the right thing. He started out at the top left hand corner and ended up at the bottom right at exactly high noon. No chances to take, no risks, just read your lines. It might be that the clergy and choir got all the good lines but they were professionals (hopefully) and one could be secure in confidence that nothing unexpected or chancy would happen in worship. It was all very respectable.

I believe during the first half of this period that worship came to be understood as largely an aesthetic experience by many ministers and lay people. Probably the most representative book of this period was Von Ogden Vogt's, *Art and Religion,* published in 1921 and subsequently in 1929, 1948, and 1960.[3] The title itself is indicative. Pastor of a Unitarian church in Chicago for two decades, Vogt was vigorously opposed to creedalism and dogmatism of any kind, and could anticipate many of our contemporaries in defining "worship as the celebration of life," by advocating a "substitute scripture reading taken from modern sources," and through using a variety of art forms. The experience of beauty and the experience of religion seemed remarkably similar to him. The arts served to help the worshiper "to be reverent and to display to him the larger cause of religion." [4] Vogt advised ministers to select "from the materials of the past those treasures which are least burdened with abandoned concepts." [5]

For many, public worship became an art form itself. Tremendous efforts were made in raising the "quality" of church music. A growing concern about church architecture was reflected in the creation of denominational building agencies. The use of classical prayers instead of spontaneous ones increased considerably. Books were written on "the art" of public worship.[6]

The warm glow of the conversion experience (or its memory) had been replaced for many by the more refined thrill of aesthetic experience. Here there was no risk of spontaneous emotion, no danger of exposing oneself by outward commitment. It was worship in good form, in which nothing overmuch prevailed. It was, in short, middle-class America with its primary values of security and comfort. Worship could continue to be a meaningful, though highly subjective experience, without the risks of self-disclosure that revivalism demanded. If you could no longer tap your feet to the music, you could no longer do a lot of things in the big city that you did back in small-town America. So once again the worship tended to mirror the values of the prevailing culture.

But the culture did not stand still and neither did the forms of our worship. The years after World War II saw a quite different interest in worship in which the dominant phrase was "recovering our heritage," a phrase not without self-contradictions. I remember how much this era troubled Vogt, how much he regarded it as regression to a dark age of creedalism and dogmatism. It still remained a period of respectability both in worship and in American culture in general. But the thrust in worship was quite different and aestheticism came to be looked at with real suspicion.

It must be remembered that the late 40s and 50s were a period of great growth in the American churches, a tendency that lost momentum in the 1960s. Attempts were frequently made, and with some justice, to connect this growth in church membership with the age of anxiety. Americans were learning to live at the center of the stage of world politics, we were learning to live with the atomic bomb, we had to live with sputnik. In theology, neo-orthodoxy emphasized man's sinfulness and offered us in turn a high Christology.

It is not surprising that aestheticism hardly seemed sufficient to those distraught by postwar anxieties. All around there was a search for more secure foundations. The "recovering of our heritage" that flourished for a quarter of a century in worship now seems to have been a necessary and vital stage, though, I believe, one we have now gone beyond. We should not be surprised that two of the elements in worship that tended to be stressed were those of confession and creed. The fascination with confession was no accident; no one who lived through World War II could have much doubt about man's sin. Professor Perry Miller once said he was an Emerson man till he led the tank corp that liberated Buchenwald; from then on he was a Jonathan Edwards man. Certainly we went to some excesses in stressing confession during this period just as our predecessors had neglected it. And the creeds gave us something firm to stand on, a need we felt greatly.

We turned to the historians for more foundations. Bard Thompson's *Liturgies of the Western Church* [7] may well stand as the representative book of this period. It should be noticed that while he did pay homage to the ancient and medieval church, the great bulk of the book is devoted to Reformation liturgies and no space to the Eastern liturgies. This was characteristic of our interests at that time. We were rediscovering Bucer, not Hippolytus then. Presbyterians were re-examining Calvin and Knox, Methodists were beginning to recognize Wesley, and Lutherans were taking a new look at the early Lutheran agendae. Names such as W. D. Maxwell, J. E. Rattenbury, Luther Reed, and others stood out. Dix's *Shape of the Liturgy* [8] was recognized in some of its aspects while others had to await a subsequent period. The reformers were rediscovered with a bit of shock due to the belated realization of how much the nineteenth century had separated us from them.

One could argue that the rediscovery of confession with its emphasis on man's weakness and the indulgence in creeds with their threat of dogmatism signaled the end of the enlightenment in worship as much as the age of anxiety did in culture in general. The comfortable pew still remained but something was rattling the clouds overhead and we had to find a substance in our worship that we had previously neglected.

But something happened in the late 1960s and early 1970s to American culture and we are just beginning to see what it implies for our worship. It may be premature to recognize the significance of these changes but I think of them as the splintering of society. Whereas a decade ago we had a well-agreed image of what the good life in America consisted of, it would be hard to find any unanimity on that today. The conformity of the past with regard to life styles, morality, proper dress, hair styles, almost anything you can name, was shattered in the 1960s. We have moved into a period of diversity, pluralism, three consciousnesses, or whatever label you use. This has not been without shock and conflicts as the old conformities came toppling down.

The cultural changes have been reflected in worship by the move to a pluralistic approach. I would attribute most of the recent changes in worship to the attempt to find forms that fit the perceptual and expressive patterns natural to a wide variety of people. We have recognized, belatedly perhaps, that those forms that appeal to a middle-class group in their mid-forties may strike their children as unrelieved dullness. Even devout teenagers tell us that our worship is boring because nothing happens at church. We are realizing that we have, in effect, told children that they must behave as adults in order to worship. It is okay to be a child 167 hours a week but never on Sunday at eleven o'clock. That is the time to sit still and listen to someone talking literally and figuratively over one's head. Hopefully we are now beginning to hear what Dix meant when he said worship is far more than words.

In this pluralistic approach to worship we have rediscovered some of the things that revivalism knew. We need to know and understand people in order to plan Christian worship. We need to take seriously the importance of the whole body and all the senses in worship and to recognize that music is a body art. We need to sense the importance of spontaneity and its advantages over a professionally conducted and controlled service as smooth as butter. It is no wonder that so-called contemporary worship services seem to appeal especially to the long-haired crowd and the grey-haired crowd.

Our society is mixed. In almost every congregation there are folks who want to sing the "old" hymns (i.e., those of revivalism), people who want to sing the "good" hymns (i.e., those which are in good taste) and persons who want to sing "something that moves" (i.e., those songs which have a "beat"). I would submit that none of these is more Christian or more adequate than any of the others. We must learn to think of our church music in terms of being "good for" whom, not in abstract terms of quality. When I fretted at a small town congregation for not singing Ralph Vaughn Williams' "Sine nomine" I forgot that what was "good for" a seminarian might not be "good for" California ranchers.

The "in" word in worship these days is indigenization. Vatican II underscored the need to make "legitimate variations and adaptations to different groups, regions, and peoples, especially in mission lands." [9] But suddenly we have found that the real problem of indigenization is right here at home. How do we devise forms of worship in which children can take "that full, conscious, and active participation in liturgical celebrations *which is demanded by the very nature of the liturgy*"? [10] Or how can youth fulfill their priesthood best? Or what of us middle-aged folks who want nothing that involves much risk but would like some real substance?

I would say that we see basically three models developing in an effort to develop worship forms natural to the way a variety of people perceive and express what is ultimately real for them. The first of these models I call "eclectic." It is the type of service which is carefully planned to reflect a cross section of the congregation. In the prayers appear the anxieties of both liberals and conservatives, the music varies from gospel song to Bach to folksong or further, and the language ranges from Cranmer to Malcolm Boyd. Purists decry this type of polyglot service but it has advantages. It certainly demands that the pastor and worship committee know the people to whom they are ministering.

The second emerging pattern is the occasional service in which on certain Sundays the whole service is in a style congenial to a particular segment of the congregation. This may mean a youth Sunday once a month. This has some advantage to the purist and also is easier to plan and staff. But it is also easier to skip if one feels he's not in the group primarily involved unless, of course, the style of each service is not announced in advance. These first two patterns are possible in churches of any size.

A third pattern seems to be current in many large congregations. This is the multiple service route. A number of different styles and occasions of worship are offered. Frequently they occur in different spaces and at different hours. One goes where he feels most natural. Such a system is rather difficult to staff and populate except in large congregations but it has received favorable responses in a number of these. In effect, it means the development of communities within a larger congregation. I have been part of one such group for over three years now.

Not all attempts at these three models have been successful by any means. But they do seem to be some indication of where we are moving in worship in 1973. The fact that the ILCW communion service first appeared with four musical settings, as varied as chant and folksong, is a sign of the times. The pluralistic approach comes not without difficulties but there is good precedent for being all things to all people in order to serve them well. We have seen important changes in our culture; our worship is reflecting these too. And as our culture changes in the future, we can likewise expect changes in the forms of Christian worship.

Christian Worship: A Formal Definition

You will recall we began by citing Vatican II in its contrast of the unchangeable elements of worship and those subject to change. After such a quick run through the multitude of changes that have occurred in Protestant worship during the past century, we may be wondering about those unchangeable elements. I am convinced that defining the permanent and immutable elements of worship is one of the prime questions before the church today. Much experimentation has been irresponsible and fruitless because it has neglected to define what is essential and immutable in Christian worship. There have been books that encourage people to think that excitement and entertainment alone justify almost any type of liturgical experimentation. A return to the crude pragmatism of revivalism is all too evident when services are evaluated as to how much they stir up people. This, I submit, is no basis on which to judge Christian worship.

What then is Christian worship? I think we can begin with what happens first: we assemble. But assembly is far from enough, especially, as Paul warns us, if we fail to discern the body (1 Cor. 11:29). The most obvious and yet easily missed fact about discerning the body is that it must be a common act, something done together. Yet the Corinthians missed this by not waiting for one another and by not considering each other. It may be that the most important single thing about worship is that it is done by the Christian assembly. We meet, assemble, come together, gather, congregate as those called out to assemble in Christ's name.

But the assembly for Christ has a purpose. We come together, deliberately seeking to approach reality at its deepest level by becoming aware of God in and through Jesus Christ and by responding to this awareness. Assembly with such a deliberate and communal expectation of awareness and response would seem to be normative for Christian worship, whatever the forms used may be. An occasion may be edifying, exciting, entertaining but I would not deem it Christian worship, unless the deliberate seeking, the awareness, and the response were present.

Our definition needs further probing. Christian worship is not an accidental occurrence but a deliberate probing in depth beneath the obvious and superficial. This is no escape from the world but an attempt to be with the world in the full seriousness it deserves rather than simply with the top layer of our consciousness. One can hardly expect to worship without trying to penetrate beyond the obvious in life. To see merely a collection of people in a church building rather than recognizing those called out to assemble for Christ is surely the same as failing to discern the body by being a glutton in Corinth.

Becoming aware of God in and through Jesus Christ does not mean receiving new information but the rediscovering of what we already know and constantly forget. One could speak of it equally well as reconsideration or recollection of past memories, particularly those shared by the community. Above all, this means the commemoration of historic events that the Christian community remembers as clues to the meaning of all history. Thus the worshipping community gathers to rehearse its corporate memories of God's acts as narrated in Scripture.

A vital part of Christian worship is the reliving of these corporate memories. I believe we can truthfully say, no anamnesis, no worship, i.e., no recalling or experiencing anew of the Christ event, no worship. In this sense, every service of Christian worship, however contemporary and relevant, involves a recalling, a remembering, a fresh experiencing of past events. Such a backward look is far from irrelevant. It may be the only way to acquire a deep insight into our relation to the world, to our neighbor, to ourselves by reconsidering them *sub specie aeternitatis*.

Now note that I am not stating what cultural form these corporate memories of the body of Christ have to take. We have celebrated the Lord's Supper without any spoken word or sound in the entire service but I am sure recollection was there. I have also seen some very moving slide shows that I would not consider Christian worship. So I am certain that his backward reference to the communities' memories, which we call Scripture, is essential to the becoming aware of God in and through Jesus Christ of which I have spoken. As long as these communal memories are rehearsed, no matter through what cultural forms, the possibility of Christian worship is present. In other terms, to qualify as Christian worship a service must express the corporate memories of the church as recorded in Scripture though it is not necessary to reproduce these memories in words. Anamnesis is certainly not limited to the forms of which we are as yet familiar.

The responses to this reawakened awareness which the body of Christ rehearses when it assembles can take many forms. The rediscovered insights demand a "so what," a fitting response: It is "meet and right so to do" something fitting for that which we have experienced again. Response, then, is a reciprocal action, concordant with the insight received. God's prior love to us is declared and we respond with our praise. Insight into our sin prompts us to confess in the hope of reconciliation. Because of our individual differences, the variety of fitting responses is large. And I suspect we will see more and more of a mix in the responses. I suspect that some will be less restrained than in the period of respectability. The witness of the Pentecostal churches represents one possible tendency, available to some. The form of responses remain varied. The chief criteria for responses are: first, that they do not interfere with others (as in eating and drinking all that is available) but rather help each other to discern the body and, secondly, that they are genuine and authentic for us as individuals. Here spontaneity can be a great asset as long as it doesn't interfere with others.

The forms of Christian worship can and will change as cultures change. But I am convinced that Christian worship will retain certain constants in its communal act of probing the depths of reality, in seeking awareness of God in and through Jesus Christ, and by responding to this awareness.

Christian Worship: A Material Definition

There is another way of defining Christian worship. We have given thus far basically a formal definition. But we can also give a material definition in which we pull together the constituent parts of Christian worship. I am firmly convinced that there are certain basic and permanent structures of Christian worship. These are those parts that "at all times, and in all places" have remained constant in Christian worship. Despite all the cultural changes of twenty centuries of time and the world-wide practice of Christian worship today in all but five countries of the globe, certain structures have been constant. Only in small groups or during brief episodes have they been eclipsed.

We must remember that the surest test of canonical literature was that it was in use throughout the Christian world. Just as Scripture provides the given though not the full details of Christian doctrine, so four structures of worship have provided the basis of Christian worship ever since the fourth century. Indeed, the roots of all four structures are earlier than Christianity itself, being derived from Jewish practices and mentalities. We may speak with Professor Massey Shepherd of a "canon" of Christian worship just as definitely as we can of a canon of Scripture.[11] The history of our worship has been elaborations of this permanent canon. Here we have a way of defining the unchanging parts of Christian worship.

The four-fold canon consists of the understanding and use of time as a means of communication, the rites of Christian initiation, the Lord's Supper, and the divine office. I shall briefly indicate how each of these structures have withstood the vicissitudes of cultural change and why I expect them to endure in the future.

The understanding and use of time as a means of communication is, of course, a direct legacy from Judaism. From Judaism comes the ability to discover God in events and in the re-enactment or remembrance of these events. Far from trying to escape time, Judaism used time to overcome time so that the worshipper could become the recipient of the saving power of past acts, no matter how far removed from them he was in time. In this sense Odo Casel spoke of us as living "our own sacred history." [12] We represent the original saving event and it becomes a part of our own internal history.

This representation works itself out in the form of the Christian day, the Christian week, and the Christian year. All become means of remembering Jesus Christ, of using time itself as a form of anamnesis. I cannot think of anything more prone to stir the imagination as we explore new forms of worship than serious consideration of the Christian calendar. The whole array of liturgical propers depends on the structures of Christian day, week, and year. In the past, some of the greatest examples of painting and music drew upon the Christian day and year for their sources.

A similar temporal character appears in our second item, the rites of initiation. For these are developed to mark a before and an after in one's relation to Christ and his church. Once we were a part of no people but through Christian initiation we have become a part of God's people. And baptism, confirmation, and first communion mark the steps by which we become a part of God's people. Initiation is a decisive act for one's self understanding as a Christian no matter whether we consciously submitted to it or not. The church has always regarded such initiation as making one a marked man for life since this decisive act imparts an indelible character.

It is not at all strange that we should signify the transition points of life by public ceremonies. Baptism and burial have much in common. At the key points in life and death actions speak louder than words. It may be that we have lost much of the dramatic sense of these occasions but there are hopeful signs we are recovering the powerful imagery of Christian initiation as the whole congregation acts out these mysteries.

It hardly seems necessary to point out the universal and enduring character of the Lord's Supper. Here again the dramatic is, or ought to be, obvious. We not only speak of the Lord's ministry but we show it forth as often as we do this. All of the senses get into the act and we plunge right to the center of salvation history.

It may be less obvious what a remarkable degree of consensus there has been in Christendom about the shape of the Lord's Supper. Four areas of common agreement as to its structure stand out with remarkable unanimity. First of all, it has two halves, the service of the word and the service of the table. Secondly, the service of the word has a persistent structure in the alternation of the recital of salvation history and praise. The third level of consensus is the basic shape of the service of the table with its four-fold actions.[13] And fourthly, there is a remarkable agreement about the contents of the second of these actions, the giving of thanks and what it ought to include.

Our fourth basic element may seem less obvious, especially to Lutherans. But the tradition of the divine office, in which the church has found a non-sacramental way of telling forth the works of Christ, underlies the worship of most of American Protestantism and is the breviary or liturgy of the hours in Roman Catholicism. Its particular genius is the ability to range through a vast amount of Scripture and especially of psalmody.

For centuries, the office has provided both a form of personal devotions and of common worship, always within the sense of the prayer of the whole church. As in the service of the word, the recitation of God's actions are joined with those of praise. Both the sober edification and the joyous praise of the synagogue are mingled in this tradition.

Frankly, I do not look for these four basic structures of Christian worship to be replaced. I look, instead, for them to continue to change in form as cultures change. Certainly they have done so for centuries past and, I am confident, will do so for centuries to come. These structures do not limit the possibilities open to us. To the contrary, they are spurs to our imagination to press on. The warm folksy Lord's Supper of the revival period (often concluding the camp meeting with a harvest of all the converted) became the rich aesthetic experience in the 1920s (with special service music) only to become the historical exercise of the newly recovered reformers' liturgies (with prayers and garb from the sixteenth century) once again to become the youth mass of the 1970s (with improvised texts and guitar music). And these in turn will give way to further cultural development of forms, perhaps largely electronic.

Thus we seek the free interplay of culture and Christian worship. The periods most to be feared are when they are too widely separated as in the freeze of Catholic worship after Trent or the lethargy of much Protestant worship in many parts of the world today. As long as the church has a clear formal and material concept of its worship, it is free to experiment. And it has much to gain as it welcomes cultural change to its worship and much to give to changing culture itself. Once we have a firm grasp on the unchangeable part of Christian worship, we are limited by nothing except the limits of our own imaginations. We who are perfectly captive are also perfectly free through Jesus Christ.

Notes

1. "Nam Liturgia constat parte immutabili, utpote divinitus instituta, et partibus mutationi obnoxiis." (Collegeville, Minn.: Liturgical Press, 1963), pp. 16-17.

2. Joe Wise, (Cincinnati: North American Liturgy Resources, 1972).

3. New Haven: Yale University Press, 1921 and 1928; Boston: Beacon Press, 1948 and 1960.

4. Rev. ed., Boston, 1948, p. 53.

5. *Modern Worship* (New Haven: Yale, 1927), p. 39.

6. Albert Palmer, *The Art of Conducting Public Worship,* (New York: Macmillan, 1939), and Percy Dearmer, *The Art of Public Worship* (London: Mowbray, 1919).

7. Cleveland: World Publishing Co., 1961.

8. Westminster, Dacre, 1945.

9. *Constitution on the Sacred Liturgy,* p. 25.

10. *Ibid.,* p. 13, (italics mine).

11. *Worship in Scripture and Tradition* (New York: Oxford University Press, 1963), p. 163.

12. *The Mystery of Christian Worship* (Westminster, Md.: Newman Press, 1962), p. 124.

13. Cf., Gregory Dix, *The Shape of the Liturgy,* pp. 48ff.

Jaroslav Pelikan

Worship
Between Yesterday and Tomorrow

This is the week of Pentecost on the Western Christian calendar —the season of the church year that embodies the theme assigned to me for this lecture: "Worship between Yesterday and Tomorrow." Pentecost is peculiarly the festival of tomorrow, the celebration of newness. Yet the form of our celebration, even of our celebration of Pentecost, is basically determined by yesterday. How do we relate yesterday and tomorrow in the worship, teaching, and life of the church? What is the rhythm of past and future? The church can thrive only if she participates in this rhythm, in what Nicephorus, patriarch of Constantinople in the early ninth century, called "the melody of theology." A disciple of St. Augustine formulated the Western Latin version of this "melody of theology" in the principle that "the rule of prayer should lay down the rule of faith." The supreme instance of this principle was, of course, the dogma of the Trinity. It is not, in the strict sense, a doctrine of the New Testament; it is, rather, the church's way of saying what it had to say to be faithful to the New Testament and to its own fundamental pattern of worship. If it was right to speak to Christ as the worship of the church did, and if the monotheism of the Bible was to be preserved, something like the dogma of the Trinity seemed to be the only way for "the rule of faith" to be conformed to "the rule of prayer" and for "the melody of theology" to be sung in harmony with both. As this was true yesterday, so it must be true tomorrow; for the church lives by the past, but for the future. Therefore she is indeed a memorial society, but not a mausoleum; and on the other hand, she can have authentic creativity in her theology and in her worship only if she overcomes the dread disease of amnesia which, especially in the modern world, doth so easily beset us all.

If the church of Jesus Christ is to be delivered both from the archaic and from the faddish, she must be able to sing the melody of theology between yesterday and tomorrow. She must do so, first of all, in her own faith, confession, and worship. When the church confesses its faith in the Creed, as we have at the Eucharist this morning, it attaches itself to the primitive confession of the primitive church, the confession of the prince of the apostles: "You are the Christ, the Son of the living God." This confession had become, well before the Gospel of St. Matthew was written, an integral part of the worship and witness of the Christian community. The ongoing development of that worship and witness eventually led the Christian community to articulate that same confession more fully in the statement of faith of the 318 fathers of the Council of Nicea, and even more fully later on. Therefore the faith of the church in all centuries is the faith confessed at Caesarea Philippi and at Nicea. Not innovation, but fidelity, is its watchword. The melody of theology, then, must never be cut off from the faithful adherence to the transmitted faith of the fathers. Whether "rock" in the words, "On this rock I will build my church," means the confession of Peter or Peter as confessor —and on this question, as you will recall, there has been some controversy—it must mean to us, at the very least, that in every age and in response to every challenge those who confess the faith of our Lord Jesus Christ are obliged, as the opening words of the symbol of the Council of Chalcedon in 451 affirm, to be "following the holy fathers."

But as the very relation between Chalcedon and its own past suggests, following the holy fathers does not mean living in the past, but living from the past and being faithful to it in facing the present and the future. The melody of theology is a song about the continuing and still expanding action of God. In response to the confession of Peter, our Lord promised: "I *will* build my church, and the gates of hell *shall* not prevail against it." The orthodox confession of the church is an expression of hope about the future, just as Pentecost is the affirmation that the selfsame Spirit conferred on the first-century church both dwells in the church and descends upon the church until the end of human history. It is interesting that at the Council of Nicea and at the Council of Chalcedon—the two great councils for the formulation of the two basic doctrines of Christianity, the doctrine of the Trinity and the doctrine of the person of Christ—the heretics were the ones who clung to old-fashioned formulas in the name of orthodoxy, as though the promise of Christ to his church meant only some golden age in the past. In the debates over Nicea, it was the heretics who rejected the homoousion because it had not been used before, except by Gnostics; and in the debates over Chalcedon it was the heretics who proposed that the argument be rolled back to a *status quo ante bellum*. In both cases authentic orthodoxy meant rehearsing the faith of the fathers and then drawing its implications for today and tomorrow, playing the melody of theology and then developing variations on its ancient themes. Chalcedon was "following the holy fathers" when it refused simply to parrot orthodox formularies, but went on to affirm a faith which, precisely because it was always ancient, was also always new. There is perhaps no more pressing need, amid the chaos of twentieth-century theology, than the art of singing this melody of theology, ever ancient and ever new.

Unity in the Truth

As this Conference on Worship demonstrates, the most important place for this melody of theology to be sung is in the doctrine of the church, where the relation of yesterday to tomorrow is fundamental. The church, we confess in our worship, is one, holy, catholic, and apostolic. Tying yesterday to tomorrow is, first of all, a unity in the truth of the church's doctrine. The Lutheran Reformation taught us to emphasize the centrality of teaching in the

life of the church and to insist that the unity of the church is
not primarily organizational but spiritual. A denomination that
insists that "it is sufficient for the true unity of the Christian
church that the gospel be preached in conformity with a pure
understanding of it and that the sacraments be administered in
accordance with the divine Word" is obliged continually to re-
affirm the conviction that the truth of divine revelation must
take precedence over all human ideas and systems in determining
the oneness of the church.

We have, however, tended in the Lutheran tradition to give
less attention to the demand of the New Testament that we "grow"
in the knowledge of God and that we move from yesterday to
tomorrow. Too often we have supposed that the knowledge of
God is something that the church possesses once and for all—
or, at any rate, something that our particular church has come
to possess once and for all. And we have required for the unity
of the church an acceptance of our particular and partial grasp
of the truth, which we have equated with the truth of God. As
a result we have forgotten more than once that the knowledge of
God is a dynamic and living thing, not a static and dead thing.
It is that by which and in which the church grows. As it is im-
mature and unhealthy to suppose that any one age of the church's
history has been vouchsafed the whole of Christian teaching, so
too it is presumptuous and blasphemous to assume that any one
part of the church is no longer in need of growth in the knowledge of God. From this it follows that a healthy growth demands
not only a readiness to speak, but also a willingness to hear the
truth wherever it may be present and by whomsoever it may be
spoken. The core of what Christians call the knowledge of God
is the life, death, and resurrection of our Lord Jesus Christ. Of
him the evangelist John says that "from his fullness have we all
received, grace upon grace." But not all of us have received the
same grace in the same way, and none of us possesses that fulness.
Therefore Christians grow by continuing to learn from one another.

Unity in teaching is, then, simultaneously the basis of the
church's life and its goal. As the Epistle to the Ephesians ad-

monishes, by "speaking the truth in love" we "may grow up in every way into him who is the head, into Christ." The unity of the church is a unity in Christ. He is Alpha and Omega: Alpha because the message of the church is grounded in him and in his cross; Omega because the life and history of the church, as well as the life and history of every believer, is a continuing process of change and growth into him. The worship life of the church, between yesterday and tomorrow, must give witness to this dynamic unity. We must speak the truth in love—and continue to grow up into Christ. Speaking the truth means knowing and believing it, with firmness and confidence. It does not mean supposing that we as individuals or as a church have nothing more to learn. What binds us together is simultaneously this truth-in-love and the process of growth into the truth that is in Christ. "Not as though I had already attained, either were already perfect: but I follow after, if that I may apprehend that for which also I am apprehended of Christ Jesus." The unity that the church has is a unity in that for which it has been apprehended by Christ; this is the "yesterday" of tradition and memory. The unity that the church constantly strives to find is a unity in its own apprehension of this; this is the "tomorrow" of response and responsibility. For the first of these we give thanks, for the second we pray. And in worship we look to both yesterday and tomorrow, praying that the church may become a living evidence of the first kind of unity, showing forth in its doctrine and life the oneness that God in Christ confers, and that it may also become an effectual force for the second kind of unity, manifesting, across the artificial barriers of our denominations, the oneness toward which we all press as, separately and yet together in our worship, we sing the melody of theology and name the name of Christ.

A Bond of Sanctity

The bond between yesterday and tomorrow is, second, a bond of sanctity. This is surely one aspect of New Testament teaching on which Lutherans have had to be instructed by their fellow Christians of other confessions. The Lutheran preoccupation with doctrine has sometimes managed to sever the moral nerve, or to suppose that the call to sanctity is not as important as the call to orthodoxy: right doctrine is essential, a holy life is important; but perfect doctrine without perfect life still saves, while life without doctrine is useless. Such a disjunction between doctrine and life, between unity in truth and unity in holiness, is a betrayal of the doctrine and of the worship of the church. It is a worthwhile exercise sometime to go through the collects for the Sundays and feast days of the church year with an eye on the relation of faith and holiness. For these collects, for the New Testament itself, and for the fathers and brethren of the history of the church, unity in the truth is finally and fundamentally inseparable from the holiness of the people of God.

Indeed, the message of our Lord—for whose public reading from the gospels Lutherans still rise, as they do not rise for the reading of other portions of Scripture—did not present itself in the first instance as a doctrine, not even as a doctrine about himself, but as a call to sanctity: "Repent!" Before it was over, this call to repentance implied a view of oneself and an understanding of the person of Jesus that made necessary what we call orthodox doctrine, and such doctrine was a legitimate outcome of the development. Only One who is what the worship of the church confesses him to be has the right to issue such a call to discipleship. But that was not the way the message began, and that is not the way the message has been carried in dogma and in worship throughout the centuries of history. It has, rather, been in the form of a theology with hands and feet. We have the great good fortune of living in an age when this insight has once again become an essential part of the very definition of the word "Christian." Thanks in part to the political crises in Germany and in the United States, Lutheran Christians in the twentieth century have begun to learn again the grim lesson that orthodox doctrine without holiness is a snare and a delusion, while holiness without orthodox doctrine can eventually lead to orthodox doctrine. Our Lord told this parable: "A man had two sons; and he went to the first and said, 'Son, go and work in the vineyard today.' And he answered, 'I will not'; but afterward he repented and went. And he went to the second and said the same; and he answered, 'I go, sir,' but did not go. Which of the two did the will of his father?" The one gave an orthodox answer, but failed to follow through on it in holy obedience; the other was a heretic, but a saint.

If I began to ask myself what kind of church the world will need tomorrow—indeed, what kind of church God will need tomorrow—I cannot avoid the conclusion that it will be a church in which this summons to holiness is taken with the utmost seriousness. For too long, being Christian has been equated with being conventional or being safe, worship has been equated with archaic forms, and holiness has been equated with respectability. But the heritage of the people of God, as expressed in the lives of the saints, is anything but conventional. It all began, you will recall, with one who ate with publicans and prostitutes, and who was crucified because his incandescent holiness was too much for the respectable to bear. It exploded into history at Pentecost with a phenomenon that some observers mistook for intoxication. (Can you imagine anyone mistaking a Lutheran service today for intoxication?) In a world grown cynical about the very possibility of saintliness, where everyone has a price and nothing has a value, the crying need is for an integrity and a sanctity that refuses to give in to such cynicism. Think of the institutions of our own sorry American society. One after another, political parties, public leaders, corporations, labor unions, publishers, networks, universities —and, alas, churches—have all proved to be corrupt. Is there no place where one can find a commitment that is indifferent to safety, that forgets itself and loses itself in service to the small and the poor of God's world? Can any institution withstand the corrosive power of success and safety, and take its chances with the dispossessed?

Well, if there is to be any such institution in this world, I pray and hope (though I must say that I do not always expect) that it will be the church. For the church is unique among all institutions in human history because in its very act of worship it defines its own success or failure by the simple—simple, and yet oh so complex—criterion of holiness. This means a dedication to the cause for which we pray in the Lord's Prayer: "Thy will be done on earth as it is in heaven." Within a few miles of the place where we are meeting today, there are millions of human lives being blighted forever because no ray of such holiness has ever lighted their path. The church of Christ becomes a salt that has lost its savor if the transforming power of its holiness cannot reach those lives. The yesterday of the church is the record of how, in every century and in every nation, that power has become available. If the tomorrow of the church is to be a worthy heir of that heritage, we must find new ways to sing this melody as saints and to unleash the holiness of a redeeming God upon a world in poverty and pain.

A Universality of Concern

In the melody of theology, the church brings yesterday and tomorrow together in a third way as well, in a universality of concern. The liturgies of the church have never ceased to pray for "all the churches of God" and "for all their pastors and ministers," including other churches than one's own. The worship of the church is fundamentally distorted if it fails to include in its purview the whole of the church for which Christ died. Thus the liturgies of the church have always recognized, better perhaps than its theologies, that those who have been judged worthy of the fellowship of Christ had better be worthy of our fellowship as well.

The early history of the church, as this is reflected in the Acts of the Apostles, is the account of how Christians, brought together (as we now know from the researches of such scholars as Walter Bauer) in very distinctive ways and through highly private experiences, found their way to the discovery that others had, in quite other ways and through altogether different experiences, come to the same Lord, and of how they came to affirm, often against their own prejudices, the universality of the lordship of Christ.

Repeatedly in Christian history, portions of the church universal have been tempted to suppose that their particular forms of Christian faith, life, and worship were normative for the church as a whole, and therefore to conclude that they could in effect excommunicate all their Christian brethren who did not agree with them. And repeatedly they have learned, and have had to learn, that any Christian truth that is not universal and catholic is neither Christian nor truth. The apostle Paul could write as he did because he who had had the dramatic experience of the Damascus road and his readers, whom he had never met and who had not been exposed to his other epistles, were nevertheless bound to one another in a universal communion that transcended individual forms of believing, worshiping, living, and teaching. Thus when fundamental crises hase arisen in some portion of the church, these have not been solved within the walls of one region or one monastic order or one denomination, but by the corporate discussion and collective wisdom of the Christian community as a whole: this is what we mean by an ecumenical council.

American Lutheranism will not resolve its own contemporary crises by supposing, as Job said sarcastically to his so-called friends, "No doubt but you are the people, and wisdom shall die with you." A sectarian answer to a sectarian question partakes of the worst in the question. But if, by the grace of God, the question can be seen in its larger context, then the answer too can point to such a context, nothing less than the witness and experience of the entire church, of which, not by our merit but by the generosity of the Almighty, we are privileged to be members.

If the worship of the church is to affirm today its fidelity to the yesterday and if it is to dedicate us to the tomorrow of God's people, it had better mean *all* of God's people when it says this. As Luther's exposition of the Third Article of the Creed says, it is in "the whole of Christendom on earth [die ganze Christenheit auf Erden]" that the calling, gathering, enlightening, and sanctifying power of the Holy Spirit is exercised. The great new fact of Christian history in our century (to borrow Archbishop Temple's phrase) is the discovery that this is indeed so, and that the church catholic is not, as some faint-hearted theologians of both Reformed and Lutheran persuasion have supposed, something invisible, but a vibrant reality throughout the world and throughout history.

A student of mine said to me once, "You are a gentleman and

a scholar, and there are very few of us left." Now that we have begun to recognize that there are few of us left, and that the percentage of Christians in the world is smaller today than it was yesterday and that it will be smaller each day as far into the future as we can see, the time has come when pragmatic necessity compels us to do what New Testament doctrine and the reality of the liturgy have always obliged us to do: to come to terms with the universal implications of our faith and to receive the heritage of God's people together with all of God's people in all times and in all places.

Loyalty to the Succession of the Apostles

The melody of theology between yesterday and tomorrow is, finally, a statement of loyalty to the succession of the apostles. The context of Christian worship between yesterday and tomorrow is the apostolic tradition. The worship of the church is the most evident demonstration that the apostolic tradition includes the New Testament but is not exhausted in the New Testament. The church does not study the Bible everywhere, but it does worship everywhere—in accordance with the apostolic tradition. That tradition was a powerful force long before the New Testament had ever been written, and whole centuries before it had become accepted as Holy Scripture. St. Paul could write about this tradition to the Corinthians: "I delivered unto you first of all that which I also received." It was this tradition that was put into writing in the books of the New Testament and that was affirmed by the church as its authoritative and binding canon. That canon was accepted on a variety of grounds, but common to all of them was some recognition that for the church to be the church it must be in a recognizable connection with the apostles of our Lord. Thus the Acts of the Apostles tells us, speaking of primitive Christian worship: "And they continued stedfastly in the apostles' doctrine and fellowship, and in breaking of bread, and in prayers." And in the Epistle to the Ephesians the congregation is told: "[You are] built upon the foundation of the apostles and prophets, Christ Jesus himself being the cornerstone."

Over the centuries, the church has found many different ways of showing that it was built upon the foundation of the apostles. It took a confession of faith from its baptismal worship (albeit one that did not evolve into its present form until the fourth century or so) and called it the Apostles' Creed; and even though the legend of its composition by the twelve apostles is certainly false, the intuition that called it "apostolic" was correct, for it did (and does) present the teaching of the apostles. Very early, the church identified its ministers and bishops with the apostles and saw in the letters of Paul to Timothy and Titus an expression of the conviction that every minister and bishop must be able to supply the credentials of a descent and succession from the twelve apostles. The books that eventually found their way into the New Testament were all declared to be in some sense "apostolic" even though some of them (most obviously, perhaps, the Epistle to the Hebrews) had not been composed by writers whom the church numbered among the apostles. The structure of church administration was also labeled "apostolic" in the so-called *Apostolic Constitutions,* and the *Liturgy of James* which was widely used in the Syriac-speaking East claimed to have been written by James, the apostle and the brother of Jesus. Behind the dubious historical attribution of this or that to the apostles lay the recognition that the church of Christ must authenticate itself by showing its legitimate connection with the twelve, whether with Peter as the rock and the prince of the apostles or with Andrew as the first one called or with some other apostle.

One form of connection with the twelve that has not always been emphasized in Christian history is the one embodied in the very name "apostolic." An apostle is one who has been sent forth: "As my Father hath sent me," Christ said, "so send I you." Hence one definition of the apostolic character of the church might simply be that the church is sent forth by Christ just as the apostles were. Certainly this is the part of the definition that speaks most directly to the meaning of Christian worship. "The Mass is ended. Go!" is the way the liturgy concludes. The church worships in the forms of yesterday in order to go on an apostolic errand to the world of tomorrow, to tell the story of Jesus Christ and to call men to repentance and faith. If the worship of the church is to be a responsible part of the church in action, we must devise new ways of telling this story. Our life and witness, our worship and service, must all be reflections of the apostolic tradition. Men who know nothing of Peter and Paul, James and John, must nevertheless be able to hear in what we say in our prayers and to see in what we do in our liturgy, as the Book of Acts says, that we have "been with Jesus." The ways for this to be expressed are many, and some of them cannot be imagined now. But all of them have in common the combination of service and witness, teaching and worship, that, throughout the yesterday of the church, has characterized a ministry that is loyal to apostolic tradition.

Thus the worship of the church—and this Conference on Worship—may be truly a Pentecostal event. For we can learn here what the tradition of the apostles and the fathers is, and how it has developed from their time to ours. Without this tradition we would be purblind in our effort to tell people what it means to be a believer. But this will be a treasure buried in a field unless the tradition has an opportunity to speak in its fullness, that is, unless the melody of theology rings out both as a loyalty to yesterday and as a commitment to tomorrow. If the "confessional orthodoxy" of American Lutheranism is to be truly orthodox, both in its "rule of prayer" and in its "rule of faith," the liturgy must be central to any reconstruction. It must be steeped in ancient forms and committed to the confession of the fathers, because this is the most profound inadequacy in the worship life of American Christians, whether Roman Catholic or Protestant. But it must be so deeply immersed in the tradition of yesterday that it welcomes tomorrow, liturgically and theologically, knowing that the Christ of the past is Lord of all the futures as well. We live, not, as the merchants of gloom tell us, in the "post-Christian era," but in a pre-Christian era; for he of whose treasure we have received remains inexhaustible in his riches, beckoning us from our present into his past and thus into his future. Thus we sing his melody, the melody of theology, between yesterday and tomorrow, in praise of him and in support of one another, in the ultimate hope of singing it in his eternal presence and in the nearer hope of being able, by his grace, some day to sing it all together in one holy catholic and apostolic church.

Veni Creator Spiritus.

Eugene Brand

New Accents in Baptism and the Eucharist

Baptism and the Eucharist are the two fundamental ritual acts of the Christian community. Together with verbal proclamation they form the center of gravity around which all other forms of worship orbit.

Neither Baptism nor the Eucharist sprang into the church *ex nihilo*; both have antecedents in Hebrew religion and in the broader context of religion in general. Ritual bathing in water is not peculiarly Christian, nor is the ritual of sharing of bread and wine. The form of the Baptism of Jesus—certainly one of the points of departure for Christian Baptism—was that of an initiation into the ranks of followers of a Hebrew prophet, John the Baptist. When Jesus was baptized, however, that initiatory rite was transformed by the extraordinary signs which the evangelists report.

Similarly, the Eucharist was "instituted" in the context of a Hebrew ritual meal, probably the Passover. The celebration of deliverance from Egyptian bondage was transformed by Jesus into the celebration of our deliverance from the bondage of sin. A meal of the covenant people became the meal of the new covenant. A tremendous series of overtones surrounds Baptism and the Eucharist; they are remarkably rich in significance.

Because of all this, it is appropriate to speak of new *accents*. What we are apt to call new discoveries are often facets of the action which have simply reemerged with new significance. It is important to recognize this lest the impression is created that we have at last discovered the truth while our fathers were mistaken. Since the church's infancy, such shifts in emphasis have occurred repeatedly.

I. HOLY BAPTISM

Martin Luther made Baptism fundamental in his theology, and classical Lutheran theology followed his lead. Baptism not only initiates one into the life in Christ, it also provides the ongoing dynamic for that life. Participation through baptismal waters in Jesus' death and resurrection begins the "daily dying to sin and daily rising to life" which mark the personal life of the believer. Being *in Christ* means sharing his servanthood with the so-called priesthood of all believers. Baptism, then, embodies two interrelated dynamics of the Christian life: personal forgiveness and sharing in the priestly mission of our Lord himself.

Recently we have rediscovered much of this fulness of baptismal teaching. But it has yet to come alive again throughout the church. While paying lip-service to classic baptismal theology, we have neither centered our teaching and preaching there, nor have we reflected its richness in our practice. Baptism has been slighted in favor of a "personal faith" mentality which merely reinforces the American heresy of "just me and my Jesus, we got a real good thing." The resulting view sees Baptism as a momentary event with little impact upon the life to follow. Baptisms are arranged on the phone, and little effort is made to help parents and sponsors understand what Baptism means both for the infant and for them. Larger parishes have scheduled Baptisms at times other than the community's regular worship, rather effectively obscuring the communal aspect of the sacrament. Where Baptisms do take place within the Sunday service, they are often gotten through as quickly as possible, leaving an impression of "please forgive us, folks, for impinging upon your valuable time with this little family do." Small wonder that Baptism has not been seen as important!

A. Corporate and ethical accents

Many of the new accents in Baptism are attempts to correct this
state of affairs. In some places the corrections have largely been
accomplished; in others they have not yet begun.

Except for extraordinary reasons, no one should be baptized
apart from the gathered community. Baptism is not individualistic,
though it is profoundly personal. In Baptism I come into a relationship not only with God but also with all God's other adopted
children. Their gathering and their participation must give obvious ritual testimony to that fact. Where circumstances do demand "private" Baptism, the person baptized should later be received in some obvious way into the congregation.

Our present stress that all Christians share responsibility in the
mission of the church roots in Baptism. Christian ethics, properly
understood, are baptismal ethics. Our determination to give fuller
expression to the familial or corporate nature of the congregation
roots in baptism. Christians are interrelated not because they
choose to be, but because of the "biological fact" of their Baptism. The individualistic heresy of so much of Protestantism which
has led to a perversion of the nature and mission of the church in
such areas as worship and social action finds its strongest antidote
in a robust baptismal theology.

Liturgical work on baptismal rites attempts to give clearer
expression to these aspects by: increasing the biblical imagery related to this sacrament (our present Lutheran rites had reduced it
drastically), giving the rite itself the importance befitting the
sacrament constitutive of the church, expressing more clearly
the involvement of the assembled congregation, allowing for the
more dramatically effective symbol of immersion or dipping, at-
tempting to devise one rite which can be used both with infants
and those "able to answer for themselves." The new rites also
attempt to express the continuing impact of Baptism on the shape
of the Christian life. That impact is reinforced by specific recollections of Baptism in other rites.[1]

B. Eschatological accent

The eschatological nature of Baptism is a significant new accent. In recent years we have rediscovered the eschatological character of Christianity. Such theologians as Jürgen Moltmann, Carl Braaten, and Robert Jenson continue to show us how, as Christians, we live from the future, how even the *past* events of Jesus' death and resurrection are future in their implications. In his recent *Story and Promise,* Jenson stresses the fundamental significance of *promise* to the Christian faith, that Christians live in trust that God's promises are true.

The promises we make to each other are always conditional. "The fundamental condition in all our promises is death: I cannot be held to a promise if keeping it will kill me. . . . If I am dead, what good am I to anyone, especially to the recipient of my promise? Only in destructive enterprises such as war is it otherwise." [2] But God's promise through Jesus is different. "Only a promise which had death *behind* it could be unconditional. Only a promise made about and by one who had already died for the sake of his promise, could be irreversibly a promise. The narrative content of such a promise would be death and resurrection. We are back to 'the gospel.' " [3] *We* are back to Baptism.

The function of the baptismal ritual is to connect each person with God's promise in Christ and with the community which inheres in him. Each person is made a participant in God's people and thus, by anticipation, in the promised kingdom. The victory of life over death is the Christian's hope; he lives in the assurance that the promise is true.[4] Baptism, after all, is precisely concerned with death and resurrection—our Lord's and, in him, our own.

It is this personal connection with the promise, this personal initiation into the fellowship of believers, this being sealed as God's own which is basic to understanding Baptism.

> In him (Christ) you also, who have heard the word
> of truth, the gospel of your salvation, and have be-
> lieved in him, were sealed with the promised Holy

Spirit, which is the guarantee of our inheritance until we acquire possession of it, to the praise of his glory.

Ephesians 1:13-14

. . . they (locust/scorpions) were told not to harm the grass of the earth of any green growth or any tree, but only those of mankind who have not the seal of God upon their foreheads.[5]

Revelation 9:4

Other aspects of the sacrament are implications of this fundamental change in relationship.[6] This emphasis on promise, the future, the eschatological kingdom is at least implied in Luther's *Small Catechism*:

(Baptism) signifies that the Old Adam in us, together with all sins and evil lusts, should be drowned by daily sorrow and repentence and be put to death, and that the new man should come forth daily and rise up, cleansed and righteous, to live forever in God's presence. (IV, 12)[7]

C. Baptism of Infants

The eschatologically conditioned view of Baptism gives us a solid base for the Baptism of infants. To cite only an interpretation of "all nations" in the Great Commission (Matt. 28:18-20) or of "household" (Acts 11:13-18; 16:15; 16:31-33; 18:8; 1 Cor. 1:16) is to baptize infants on ambiguous testimony. To do it because of the universality of original sin is more sound theologically, but leads easily to a quasi-magical understanding of the sacrament and/or to ignoring its communal implications.

If, however, the communal implications are taken seriously and the community being discussed is that of the promise, then it is natural for infants born into that community to be connected personally with the promise, to be sealed as God's own. Even some Baptist theologians have been impressed with this sort of justification for baptizing infants.[8] To say that infants born into the community of believers may be baptized, however, is not to support the indiscriminate practice of infant baptism which has often been practiced by the so-called historic churches. Indiscriminate infant baptism reinforces if not a quasi-magical view of Baptism, then at least a non-relational, mechanical view of grace. That, in turn, implies a "commissary" view of the church—an establishment for dispensing grace.[9]

To insist that Baptism as God's act is always effective and that we therefore should baptize every infant brought is—in the name of a truism—to evade the responsible administration of Baptism. Room must always be left, of course, for pastoral discretion. No ironclad rules can govern pastoral ministry. But we need carefully to rethink baptismal discipline in the light of the eschatological dimension of the sacrament. In doing so we need to avoid confusing Baptism with last rites.[10]

D. Christian Initiation: Baptism, First Communion, Confirmation

Communal and familial implications of Baptism also speak to the relationships between Baptism and First Communion and between Baptism and Confirmation.

This is not the occasion for a detailed history of the Rite of Confirmation nor of its relationship with Baptism. Suffice it to say that what in the early centuries was done together—baptizing in water and the Laying-on-of-Hands (with anointing)—in the Western church gradually separated into two rites. By that time infant Baptism had become the usual thing, also separating it from First Communion. A unified initiation rite—Baptism, Laying-on-of-Hands, First Communion—fractured into three components, and western Christians have had difficulties with their relationship ever since. Confirmation was condemned by Luther because, as a sacrament, it was judged to have no biblical justification. There was general agreement, however, that some form of instruction should precede First Communion. Motivated pedagogically, Confirmation gradually returned.[11] Eventually the pattern stabilized among Lutherans and other Reformation churches: 1) Baptism in infancy, 2) Confirmation at puberty preceded by special instruction, 3) First Communion following Confirmation.

Recently, Lutheran educators have objected to this pattern. Their objections are neither within my competence nor the scope of this paper. Even on other grounds, however, the pattern of preceding First Communion with a rite of Confirmation does precisely what Luther found so objectionable: the impression is unavoidable that Confirmation adds something lacking in Baptism—something needed before one is a full, communicant member of the fellowship. It implies that baptized persons are not full members of the church, a position impossible to defend. It further implies, of course, that full membership depends on intellectual credentials (instruction and catechetical examination preceding Confirmation).

All baptized persons must be recognized as having the privilege, as members of the family, of the family table. In Orthodox churches this is underlined by including infants in the communion immediately following their Baptism. But my affirmation does not *necessarily* imply such a measure. Some aspects of family life relate to one's maturity. Families do not regard babies as only partial members, but they usually do not feed them at the table until they are mature enough to observe minimal amenities. Some foods and beverages are not permitted children until certain ages, though this varies greatly according to the culture. What I am getting at is this: nothing should be done to imply that a baptized infant is only a partial member of the church though some privileges of membership may remain potential rights until certain levels of maturity have been reached. When the level has been reached, however, the privileges should be enjoyed without interposing a juridical ceremony—especially not a rite which carries sacramental force (whether called a sacrament or not).

Growing understanding in the infant member results from interpersonal experience just as much—maybe more—as from more formal, programmed learning. When a simple awareness dawns that relationships with God and other people imply mutual obligations, the child is surely mature enough to participate in the Eucharist. Most children reach this point rather early—long before the fifth grade! I have heard six-year-old children express an "understanding" of the Lord's Supper—in simple terms of relationship—which would put many adults to shame. When that point is reached and some simple teaching has occurred, let the children naturally accompany their parents to the altar for their First Communion.

If, in mid-adolescence, there is an intensive period of instruction which culminates in a public rite, that rite should be no more (or no less!) than a remembrance of Baptism and perhaps an open declaration of continued commitment to the church's mission. It must not imply entrance into the fullness of membership as if something was lacking before.

Lutherans have a tremendous task of reorientation ahead of them on the whole matter of Christian initiation. Indeed, it has already begun. But unless it is based on different theological premises than those now employed officially, only greater confusion can result. To oversimplify: at the heart of it is whether Christianity is regarded primarily as corporate (suggesting the norms of family life) or as individualistic (suggesting the norms of voluntary groups). This is especially tricky for American and Canadian Christians. We all too easily confuse our decision to become a member of a particular parish or denomination with becoming a Christian. The former is somewhat voluntary and based on individual preference; the latter is not. The church of Christ is not a voluntary group which I simply decide to join.

E. Baptism and Mission

Finally, Baptism is a kind of ordination. The baptismal font is the womb of the one-class society called the church where all are equal before God as brothers and sisters in Jesus Christ. This fellowship is "ordained" to proclaim the good news of God in Christ and to exemplify in its very being God's plan for his creation.

To say that the whole church is Christ's mission does not mean that each member has the same function. St. Paul's figure of the *body of Christ* helps us there. Within the body there is a presi-

dential ministry which is part of God's plan for the church. This
special ministry carries the responsibility for proclaiming the
gospel in the church and presiding at the Eucharist and other
rites of the whole community. Such a "ministry of word and
sacrament" (a convenient if theologically misleading phrase) is
related to the ministry of the apostles. Because this ministry deals
with those instrumentalities God has chosen to create and maintain the fellowship, it is fundamental to the church's existence.
But there are other ministries also without which the church
cannot properly fulfill her mission: teaching, music and the arts,
social service, healing, administration, and countless others not
so easy to label.

Some ministries, such as the ministry of word and sacrament,
are primarily related to the life of the church itself. Their function is to enable people to grow and become sensitive to their
responsibilities, and to guard the authenticity of the church's life
and teaching. Some ministries, such as that of social service, are
primarily focused outside or beyond the life of the church itself.
Both sorts must be vital and competent if Christ's mission is to
go forward. The attitude often current today that any Christian
can perform any service is eventually destructive of all ministries.
That omni-competence and omni-responsibility is not true of other
forms of society; it is not true of the church. Baptism should
lead us to a vision of unity of purpose and diversity of function
in which each person can fulfill his ministry. He can fulfill it
with joy because it's his and it suits him. He needn't worry
about its rank or status. Baptism viewed as ordination permits no
one, however, to escape the obligation of ministry.

II. THE HOLY EUCHARIST

More words have been spoken and written about the Lord's
Supper than about all the other actions of the church put to-
gether—devotional words, theological words, argumentative words.
That is really not surprising when one notices how the whole of
the Christian faith focuses in this simple meal of bread and wine.
Controversies in the Reformation and since have resulted on all

sides in lopsided theological viewpoints. The recent renaissance of biblical studies and the ecumenical and liturgical movements have focused on the Eucharist. The result has been a measure of consensus across frontiers that only a generation or so ago seemed permanently closed.

Unfortunately this consensus has sometimes been of the least-common-denominator variety motivated more by sentiment than by struggle with the issues. But most often it has been achieved by hard work. Research has resulted in greater knowledge both of the Scriptures and of the church's theological tradition. On that basis it has been possible to transcend the terms of past debates which had been deadlocked for centuries. It is conceivable, for example, that the famed Marburg Colloquy would have turned out differently if Luther and Zwingli had had access to our knowledge of the Scriptures and the Fathers.[12]

As with Baptism, much of the recent thinking about the Eucharist relates to the shift from an individualistic to a corporate viewpoint. This shift has been motivated by the rediscovery of the nature of the church itself. It is not primarily hierarchy, or clergy, or bureaucratic structure; it is the people of God and the body of Christ. St. Paul's use of the latter figure both for the Eucharist and for the church indicates their intimate relationship.

Restoring the Eucharist to its natural place in the center of corporate life presents the various churches with differing problems. Roman Catholics, for example, could take regular celebrations of the Eucharist for granted, but not frequent communion of the people. Lutherans, on the other hand, had fewer celebrations, but more people communing at each one. In both churches the Eucharist was dominated by the clergy; the people saw their role as subordinate. Whether celebrated daily or quarterly, a few communions a year seemed sufficient because reception was thought of almost completely in individualistic terms.

Roman Catholics seem to have made greater progress in this. Already having the Mass each Sunday, and having a Eucharist-centered piety makes their problem primarily one of reorientation. This would be true also, I assume, for a good portion of Episcopalians. Lutherans and other Protestants could count neither on a Eucharist every Sunday nor on a Eucharist-centered piety. Therefore there are more barriers for us.

This is the place to stress that by Eucharist, I mean a liturgy which includes the reading and exposition of the Scriptures, intercession, and the meal-action itself.

A. Accent on Thanksgiving

Foremost among the new accents is the recovery of the spirit of thanksgiving that led early Christians to call their paschal meal Eucharist. As the result of medieval piety and of the terms of the Reformation protest, the main accent had been—at least among Lutherans—the forgiveness of sins. Luther's *Small Catechism* teaches that the benefits of sacramental eating and drinking are expressed

> in the words "for you" and "for the forgiveness of
> sins." By these words the forgiveness of sins, life,
> and salvation are given to us in the sacrament, for
> where there is forgiveness of sins, there are also life
> and salvation. (VI, 6) [13]

That is a splendid statement if one understands, as Luther did, that forgiveness of sins leads to a life filled with the hearty joy of salvation. But Lutheran sacramental piety developed along rather more lugubrious lines so that the mood of the Lord's Supper was more appropriate to Yom Kippur than Passover. Added to this was an intense individualism which almost refused to acknowledge the presence of other communicants: "*I* go to communion when *I* need it for the forgiveness of *my* sins." That is not wrong, but it is terribly lopsided. Communion was a somber experience of the cross with almost none of the joy of the resurrection.

We are rediscovering the solemn joy that actually pervades the Eucharist: joy both in Christ's victory and in the gathering of the fellowship. We are beginning to understand why the shared loaf is more eloquent a symbol than paper-thin, tasteless wafers. We are beginning to grasp the significance of sharing the cup of wine—

the beverage of celebration. We respond to positioning the table to allow the presiding minister to function naturally in the role of host and us to gather around the family board. We see the value and propriety in involving several people—including laity—as assisting ministers in leadership roles to give fuller symbolic expression to the gathered community.

All this represents a recovery of those features of the shared meal which disappeared one by one as the Eucharist became more clericalized. Robert Hovda describes it:

> The priest usurped the deacon's role. The priest usurped the lector's role. The priest usurped (often enough) the acolyte's role. He usurped the role of presenting the gifts. He usurped part (and sometimes all) of the musicians' roles. In congregations of fair or large size, he usurped the roles of other ministers of holy communion. He usurped the role of maker of parish announcements. Except for unisonal things, he was usually the sole vocal pray-er and always the sole vocal preacher. He even usurped the role of the congregation, at least as far as any vocalization was concerned.
>
> . . . only when the rich variety of ministerial roles is clear in the act of worship, will the congregation as a whole get out of its psychological "adversary" role and into the common task at hand.[14]

The clericalization of the Eucharist parallels the modifications which enveloped the liturgy and piety of the Western church in the early Middle Ages.[15] Its clericalization also fits the Eucharist neatly into the "commissary" view of the church as dispenser of grace. Corporate celebration and eucharistic joy go hand in hand, one is difficult without the other.

We must, of course, admit that misguided attempts at celebration have cheapened the Eucharist by reducing it to little more than a social occasion. Foot-tapping rhythms and hand-holding togetherness will not produce true eucharistic joy (though both *may* be legitimate expressions of it). The Eucharist is not a mere celebration of life or of creation; it is a celebration of the new life in the new world we anticipate in Christ. There's a vast difference. A valid and needed emphasis upon the corporate dimension must not displace the necessary emphasis upon the "transcendent" dimension. Solemn joy, joy tinged with awe in the face of God's mystery—that is the stance of true celebration.

B. Accent on Sacrifice

Sacrifice is a second new accent. The popular concept of the sacrifice of the mass was the target of the Reformation's most vivid polemic. The terms of the argument were such that it could not be resolved. People had perverted the concept of sacrifice with all sorts of sub-Christian notions. In the name of the gospel, the Reformation so over-reacted, however, that a proper and biblical sacrificial position became impossible on both sides.

Careful studies have now differentiated the pious perversions of the pre-Reformation period from the more responsible theological tradition. Biblical studies especially have clarified and enriched our understanding of the sacrificial concepts of Hebrew religion and their impact upon the language of the New Testament. We therefore have been given new insights to deal with the Reformation controversy.

One aspect is a resolution of the typically Lutheran question, Is worship *sacrificium* (our offering to God) or *beneficium* (God's gift to us)? Actually, of course, it's both. Christians would have called Hebrew sacrifices sacraments. Ostensibly worship is our obedient response to what God has made us; we do the things he has commanded with words, water, bread and wine. "In, with, and under" these actions of ours God acts upon and through us. This truth is at the root of our understanding of Baptism and the Eucharist after all. God's action and our action dare not be confused, but neither can they be separated.[16]

To use the language of Philippians 2, it is part of the gracious condescension of God that he speaks to us through human language and works among us through human actions. Those who speak and act do so as an offering or sacrifice of obedient service; those who hear and receive, perceive God at work through human agents.

The same situation relates to the Eucharist itself. The Eucharist can be called sacrifice in two senses: 1) The sacrifice of praise which we make as we proclaim the gospel and share the meal is our obedient response through which God in Christ is present and active among us. In this sense the Eucharist is both sacrifice and sacrament; 2) Sharing the bread and wine proclaimed to be Christ's body *given* and his blood *shed*, is sharing in the benefits of his sacrifice. As Peter Brunner has pointed out, we should not limit our concept of Jesus' self-offering to the cross, though that is where it climaxes. Jesus' sacrifice encompasses his whole life of service to the Father which he offered freely for us.[17] All this we receive as we receive his body, as we share in his sacrifice.

The great strides toward resolving the Reformation controversy about sacrifice are obvious from the excerpts of a joint statement issued by participants in the Roman Catholic-Lutheran dialogues:

> Lutherans and Roman Catholics alike acknowledge that in the Lord's Supper 'Christ is present as the Crucified who died for our sins and who rose again for our justification, as the once-for-all sacrifice for the sins of the world who gives himself to the faithful! (COCU: Principles) On this Lutherans insist as much as Catholics. . . .
>
> The confessional documents of both traditions agree that the celebration of the eucharist is the church's sacrifice of praise and self-offering or oblation. . . .[18]

A recent report on the international Lutheran-Roman Catholic working group spoke of "achievement of a breakthrough towards an understanding of the Eucharist as 'sacrifice' which not only eliminates traditional Lutheran reservations in decisive points, but even corresponds to the Lutheran doctrine on the Eucharist in important aspects." [19]

This new accent on sacrifice is behind the offertory prayer in the provisional liturgy for Holy Communion of the Inter-Lutheran Commission on Worship, and also these words from the Great Thanksgiving:

> Gracious Father, we therefore celebrate the sacrifice of our Lord by means of this holy bread and cup: rejoicing to receive all that he accomplished for us in his life and death, his resurrection and ascension. . . .[20]

C. Accent on Real Presence

Growing consensus on the theology of the real presence is the third new accent in the Eucharist. The Reformation argument on this point was more between the Lutheran and Swiss reformers than between Lutherans and Rome. Article 10 of the *Augsburg Confession* is an unequivocal statement of the real presence and this article was uncontested in the *Confutation*. The *Apology* reaffirms the stand in even stronger language, adding the word *substantial* (Art. 10, Latin text). Transubstantiation is rejected by Lutherans not because of what it affirms, but because it attempts to explain the real presence, and does it in a way that is open to gross popular misinterpretations. Lutherans object further to being tied to the philosophical categories it employs.

Roman Catholic theologians have recently put forward new expressions of the real presence doctrine. They stress a change in the meaning and reality of the bread and wine rather than a change in substance (substance, for us, suggests a chemical change—not at all what the classic doctrine intended). Dutch theologians Edward Schillebeeckx and Piet Schoonenberg have been the influential voices.[21] *Transignification* affirms a change in the sign character of bread and wine in the Eucharist. They become effective signs of Christ's presence. *Transfinalization* is a similar concept though its emphasis is upon the new purpose or value which bread and wine acquire in the Eucharist. Transignification and Transfinalization affirm that the bread is Christ's body not because of any chemical change which has occurred, but because of its symbolic value and its ultimate purpose; the bread has, in other words, changed in its relationship to the worshipers.

I mention these theological concepts here because they indicate a new flexibility in interpreting transubstantiation that Lutherans especially should find appealing. As Paul Jersild has recently observed:

> Lutherans have always been suspicious of the word 'change' in the Eucharist, rejecting the change expressed in the doctrine of transubstantiation. . . . The Lutheran rejection of a change maintains the sign-value of bread and wine: the reality of Christ is received "in and with" the elements, which remain bread and wine. Schillebeeckx and Schoonenberg also maintain the sign-value of the elements throughout the act, but in their participation in the reality of Christ's presence, they become the body and blood of Christ for the congregation of believers. This understanding of change should be acceptable to Lutherans, for it does not contradict the Lutheran thesis that the bread and wine remain the same as far as their chemical make-up is concerned, at the same time as they become the body and blood of Christ in the sacrament.[22]

The Roman Catholic-Lutheran dialogue found disagreement only on the questions of the extension of the presence and of adoration of the reserved sacrament.[23]

In international conversations between Anglicans and Lutherans, agreement was noted on the doctrine of the real presence as well as the relationship between the Eucharist and Christ's sacrifice.[24]

Historically, the argument on the real presence has been between Lutherans and the Reformed Churches. After a common reexamination of the Scriptures in the light of modern biblical research, German Reformed and Lutheran churchmen produced the so-called Arnoldshain Theses on the Lord's Supper (1958). The heart of the statement on Christ's presence is Thesis IV:

> The words which our Lord Jesus Christ speaks when
> he offers the bread and the cup tell us what he him-
> self gives to all who come to this supper: he, the
> crucified and risen Lord, permits himself to be taken
> in his body and blood given and shed for all, through
> his word of promise, with the bread and wine, and
> grants us participation, by virtue of his Holy Spirit,
> in the victory of his lordship, so that we, believers in
> his promise, may receive forgiveness of sins, life and
> salvation.[25]

Thesis V sharpens the statement with a series of disclaimers.

By comparison, the summary statement from the U.S. Reformed-Lutheran conversations seems less substantial:

> 6. When by word is meant the proclamation of the
>   gospel, the sacrament is a form of visible, enacted
>   word through which Christ and his saving bene-
>   fits are effectively offered to men. Accordingly,
>   the sacrament is a means of grace . . .
>
> 8. We are agreed that the presence of Christ in the
>   sacrament is not effected by faith but acknowl-
>   edged by faith . . .
>
> 9. The significance of christology for the Lord's
>   Supper is that it provides assurance that it is the
>   total Christ, the divine-human person, who is pres-
>   ent in the sacrament, but it does not explain how
>   he is present.[26]

On the basis of these conversations, however, the participants rec-ommended to their churches that they "enter into discussions look-ing forward to inter-communion and the fuller recognition of one another's ministries" because they saw "no insuperable obstacles to pulpit and altar fellowship." [27]

On both historic fronts, Lutherans and their former opponents have discovered a high degree of consensus on the doctrine of the real presence. It should not surprise us, then, when great similarities are noted in books on the Eucharist nor, indeed, when recent eucharistic liturgies proposed by the various groups mentioned evidence a great measure of similarity.[28]

D. Accent on Eschatology

Finally, there is the accent on eschatology. Much of what was stated about eschatology under Baptism is applicable here also. The forward-look is present in the New Testament in three ways: 1) The gospel narratives of the scene in the upper room quote Jesus as saying "I shall not drink again of this fruit of the vine until that day when I drink it new with you in my Father's kingdom." [29] Following the imagery of the Apocalypse, Christians have seen the Eucharist as a foretaste or an anticipation of the "marriage supper of the Lamb." 2) Reports of the post-Easter appearances of Jesus contain meal references. Both in the Emmaus scene (Luke 24:13-35) and the breakfast by the Sea of Tiberius (John 21:4-14), there is direct reference to the breaking or giving of bread. While it may be excessive to see the Eucharist behind every crumb of bread in the New Testament, scholars seem agreed that the Eucharist must be set in the entire meal-context of the gospels.[30] Meals reported in the post-resurrection appearances underline the eschatological thrust. 3) The connection of the Eucharist with Jesus' death and resurrection also have future implications, since these events usher in the kingdom which will be fully realized at the last day.

The eschatological accent in the Eucharist strengthens hope in the promise that the kingdom has and shall come; the Eucharist becomes a foretaste of the perfect fellowship of that kingdom.[31]

> As we represent Jesus' table fellowship with his first followers, we anticipate the final fellowship that he will establish to include both them and us. The oldest prayer at the Eucharist is "Come, Lord Jesus!" Thus the word that commands this recollection is itself shot through with promise: "This is my body," is a promise of his presence when the meal is eaten. He gives up his body and sheds his blood not by mis-

chance, but for a purpose, "for" us. The cup promises the "new covenant" of Isaiah and Jeremiah; and
is a declaration of "forgiveness," of the new future
in spite of the past.[32]

Here is the antithesis to the "commissary" view of the church.
Eller calls it the "caravan" view.[33] It opposes a view of the church
as a vast distribution center of grace with a more biblical view of
the church as the pilgrim people of God under way from resurrection to parousia, from Baptism to death/resurrection. The eucharistic meal then becomes not an individual drawing upon the store of
grace, but a shared celebration of who God has made us in Christ,
a strengthening of our trust in his promise, and thus an enabling
of our mission among humankind. That is what remembrance of
Jesus' death and resurrection and anticipation of his perfect kingdom are all about. Once caught, that orientation will turn the meal
into a true Eucharist and save it from the legalism and the lugubri-
ousness of the "commissary" mentality.

III. CHRIST, CHURCH, SACRAMENTS

It is sound Lutheran practice to arrive at "the sacraments" in-
ductively rather than to begin with a definition of *sacrament* and
proceed deductively to Baptism, the Eucharist, and other churchly
rites.[34] While definitions are useful, they can be procrustean—especially in this case since *sacrament* is not a biblical term. The induc-
tive procedure also prohibits positing the unity of these rites in an
arbitrarily defined category—even if the definition has centuries of
tradition behind it.

A. Unity in the Word

Reformation theology in general and Lutheran theology in particular have seen the unity of ritual actions in the Word. Word is
more than biblical words, liturgical words or sermon words. Word
is the living voice of the gospel perceived and received in and
through such words. Word is also the living voice of the gospel in

Baptism and the Eucharist. Word, then, is a dynamic concept; it refers to God at work. Biblically, of course, Word is used for Christ who is the incarnate Word. (It is this fulsome concept of Word that makes our habitual phrase "word and sacraments" misleading because the phrase implies that sacraments are something other than word.)

Word relates God's activity in the world through Jesus, the church, verbal proclamation, and the sacraments.[35] It links these revelations of God together by giving them a dynamic center. It indicates the continuity of the mission of Christ with the mission of his people, the church. It ties together the chief instruments in the church's mission: teaching/preaching, Baptism and the Eucharist. The church and the so-called means of grace are all human, earthly instruments in and through which God is present and active.

This sort of thinking allows the Lutheran Confessions to be somewhat freewheeling about the use of *sacrament*.[36] Evangelically conditioned ears should not find it strange, for example, to hear the church called "the sacrament of unity." What Reformation theology has affirmed about preaching makes it sacramental. The various actions share a function as symbols bearing the active presence of God.[37] God's presence does not make the words or water or bread become divine; such a change would nullify their function as symbols. Proclamation, Baptism and the Eucharist are symbolic actions where, because of his promise, we can expect to find God at work, but God may be perceived in other actions as well (e.g., a comforting touch, a struggle for justice, a protest against inhumanity, a prayer for peace).

B. Unity in Sacramentality

Roman Catholic theologians have been expanding their use of *sacrament* and making "sacramentality" the unifying concept.[38] *Sacrament* is understood as symbolic action in and through which God in Christ is present and active. Thus Christ is called the *proto-sacrament* (the model of sacrament) and the church is the *primordial sacrament* (the fundamental sacrament). Such terminology attempts to show the close relationship between the mission of Christ and that of the church.

Jesus is the revelation of God's purpose for the world; his mission accomplishes that purpose. The church is a sign or symbol of God's purpose for the world—to unite humanity as one body in Christ (Ephesians 3:4-6, 8-12)—the sacrament of the salvation and unity of all mankind.[39] The pilgrim people show—or should show—that this unity already exists by the sort of catholicity which transcends racial, economic, sexual and national barriers.

Baptism, the Eucharist, and the other sacraments are then seen as specific instruments of the church's life and purpose. *Sacramentality* describes the common relationship of God's activity in the world through Jesus, the church, and the sacraments.[40] Our discussion of transignification and transfinalization showed new efforts to preserve the true symbol-character of the sacraments—i.e., not suggesting that they become what they symbolize.

C. Consensus?

Using Word as the unifying concept carries the hazard of identifying Word with words as Lutheran theology amply could document. It is the hazard of intellectualizing and thus abstracting the *dynamis* from the human context which embodies it. Using *sacramentality* as the unifying concept carries the hazard of identifying the church with Christ. It is the hazard of viewing the church as embodying the work of God without itself being confronted or addressed by it. Each concept is an effective antidote for the other.

In an article published recently in English, Karl Rahner calls for Roman Catholics to develop a theology of the Word.[41] His discussion demonstrates that the concept we have called sacramentality and the Reformation concept of the Word are open to each other. He sketches a direction which would do full justice to the relationship between Christ, the church, proclamation and the sacraments and which would be mutually acceptable to Roman Catholic and Protestant traditions. Whether or not one agrees with Rahner's solutions, the significance of a Roman Catholic theologian of his stature writing such an article is a sign of rapprochement between the two theological traditions.

Strenuous biblical, historical and theological work have brought us to the point where many of the old sacramental controversies can be resolved, where the opponent mentality can vanish, and where the lopsidedness of the individual theological traditions can find their balances. Still to be overcome is the separatism reinforced by conceiving our confessional identity in terms of negations: "We're Lutherans; that means we're not Catholics. We're Catholics; that means we're not Protestants. Etc." Such negative patterning must be faced seriously and openly where the people of God live and worship before the work of the theologians can result in significant change.

In the guise of conserving our heritage, a new spirit of isolationism threatens to reinforce the negative thinking just mentioned. If it flourishes, it will either halt or neutralize the solid theological achievements of recent decades. Reaction against the excesses and gimmickry of the sixties is rather welcome. But let it not carry away the solid work with the ephemeral putterings. In a period of conservative reaction, people of every part of our fragmented church need to affirm their fundamental unity in Christ and make an open commitment to the goal of Christian unity. This we must do not for our own sake, but for the sake of the world—because of the credibility of the gospel.

> I do not pray for these only, but also for those who believe in me through their word, that they may all be one . . . so that the world may believe that thou hast sent me.
>
> (John 17:20-21)

Notes

1. *The Services of the Word* (Contemporary Worship-5, Inter-Lutheran Commission on Worship) contain a so-called Covenant Act which employs the Apostles' Creed as a recollection of Baptism. Initial drafts of a new ILCW funeral rite contain pointed references to Baptism.

2. Robert W. Jenson, *Story and Promise* (Philadelphia: Fortress Press, 1973), p. 8.

3. *Ibid*, pp. 8-9.

4. *Ibid*, pp. 172-173. The author's calling Baptism a past-tense sacrament does not contradict what is said about living from the future.

5. For a discussion of how these passages relate to Baptism, see G. W. H. Lampe, *The Seal of the Spirit* (London: S.P.C.K., 2/1967); "In the light of what we have seen to be the New Testament doctrine of Baptism in relation to the Spirit, there can be no doubt that the decisive moment to which St. Paul refers is Baptism . . . if Baptism effects union with Christ, as St. Paul certainly claims that it does, then it is Baptism which also effects the bestowal of the Spirit" (p. 62). cf. G. R. Beasley-Murray, *Baptism in the New Testament* (Exeter: Paternoster Press, 1962-/1972), p. 174; W. F. Flemington, *The New Testament Doctrine of Baptism* (London: S.P.C.K., 1948), p. 66; and Edmund Schlink, *The Doctrine of Baptism* (St. Louis: Concordia, 1972), pp. 58-63.

6. The sort of discussion about Baptism which typically centers on original sin is not—at least in its original intention—at all antithetical to this viewpoint.

7. *The Book of Concord,* ed. Theodore G. Tappert (Philadelphia: Muhlenberg Press, 1959), p. 349.

8. E.g., Neville Clark, "Christian Initiation," *Studia Liturgica* 4:3 (1965): "Finally, infant baptism may be affirmed on the ground of the eschatological nature of the sacrament. It may be claimed that it has an inescapable proleptic element, that it inherently looks to the future for its completion, that is 'unto faith.' This is a powerful defense. It may be that upon it, at the end of the day, the case will stand—and stand firm" (p. 164).

9. Cf. Vernard Eller, *In Place of Sacraments* (Grand Rapids: Eerdmans, 1972), pp. 30ff. Using Eller's term does not imply agreement with his book though most of his criticisms must be taken seriously.

10. Jenson, p. 173.

11. For the data see Arthur C. Repp, *Confirmation in the Lutheran Church* (St. Louis: Concordia, 1964), and *Confirmation,* LWF study document, tr. Walter G. Tillmanns, (Minneapolis: Augsburg, n.d.).

12. For those with a 16th century mind-set, such ecumenical consensus inevitably seems like selling out. It is possible, however, to affirm a confessional stand taken in the Reformation while recognizing that alternatives may change in the light of greater knowledge. That is to relate dynamically rather than statically to the Reformation. The Reformers themselves, after all, took that sort of stance.

13. Tappert edition, p. 352.

14. *Living Worship* 9:5 (1973).

15. Unleavened bread became the rule in the West about the 9th century. The cup was withheld from the laity from about the 12th century.

16. Wilhelm Hahn, *Worship and Congregation,* Ecumenical Studies in Worship, 12 (Richmond: John Knox Press, 1963), p. 41.

17. Peter Brunner, *Worship in the Name of Jesus* (St. Louis: Concordia, 1968), p. 175.

18. *Lutherans and Catholics in Dialogue,* III (1967), p. 188.

19. Lutheran World Federation News Service, Release No. 11/73, p. 5.

20. Contemporary Worship—2: *The Holy Communion* (1970), p. 17. On this section of the paper, see the author's *The Rite Thing* (Minneapolis: Augsburg, 1970), chapters IV and V.

21. Schillebeeckx, *Christ the Sacrament of the Encounter with God* (New York: Sheed and Ward, 1963); *The Eucharist* (New York: Sheed and Ward, 1968) and "Transubstantiation, Transfinalization, Transignification," *Worship* 40 (1966). Schoonenberg, "Presence and the Eucharistic Presence," *Cross Cur-*

rents 17 (1967); "Transubstantiation: How Far Is this Doctrine Historically Determined?," *Concilium* 24 (1967).

22. Paul Jersild, "A Lutheran View of the Real Presence in Roman Catholic Theology Today," *Dialog* 12 (1973), p. 140.

23. *op. cit.*, pp. 191-197.

24. "Report of the International Anglican-Lutheran Conversations," *Lutheran-Episcopal Dialogue* (Cincinnati: Forward Movement, n.d.), pp. 156-157.

25. English text from *Lehrgespräch Über das Heilige Abendmahl*, ed. G. Niemeier (München: Chr. Kaiser, 1961), p. 333. cf. commentary in Eugene M. Skibbe, *Protestant Agreement on the Lord's Supper* (Minneapolis: Augsburg, 1968), pp. 69-116.

26. From *Marburg Revisited*, ed. Empie and McCord (Minneapolis: Augsburg, 1966), p. 104.

27. *Ibid*, p. 191.

28. Compare, for example, the liturgies in the COCU *An Order of Worship* (1968), the Presbyterian *Worshipbook* (1970), the Episcopal *Services for Trial Use* (1971), the *Missale Romanum* (1970), and the Lutheran *Contemporary Worship—2* (1970).

29. Matt. 26:29. (Mark 14:25, Luke 22:18, 30) cf. Acts 10:40-41, Rev. 19:9.

30. E.g., Willi Marxsen, *The Lord's Supper as a Christological Problem* (Philadelphia: Fortress, 1970), pp. 21-26; A. J. B. Higgins, *The Lord's Supper in the New Testament* (London: SCM, 1952), pp. 61-62; Oscar Cullmann, *Early Christian Worship* (London: SCM, 1953), pp. 14-17; C. F. D. Moule, *Worship in the New Testament*, Ecumenical Studies in Worship 9 (Richmond: John Knox, 1961), pp. 18-22.

31. Cf. the final chapter of *The Rite Thing*.

32. Jenson, p. 170.

33. Eller, *loc. cit.*

34. Cf. CA IX-XIII; Edmund Schlink, *Theology of the Lutheran Confessions* (Philadelphia: Muhlenberg, 1961), p. 182; Werner Elert, *Der Christliche Glaube* (Hamburg: Furche-Verlag, 5/1960), pp. 355-356.

35. Proclamation is used here and elsewhere to include preaching, witnessing, absolution, benediction.

36. Arguments about the number of sacraments have usually been pointless. It is worth noting that the Lutheran Confessions can speak of both Absolution and Ordination as sacraments. cf. Ap. XIII, 2 and 17; Ap. XII, 41; Ap. XIII, 4, 9-13, 14.

37. Symbol, as used here, means effective symbol, symbol pregnant with reality. It is not used as it was in Reformation polemics.

38. E.g., E. Schillebeeckx, *op. cit.*, especially pp. 5-45; Karl Rahner, "What Is a Sacrament?" *Worship* 47 (1973), pp. 274-284; Nicholas Lash, *His Presence in the World* (London: Sheed & Ward, 1968), especially pp. 151-154.

39. Cf. *Lumen Gentium:* I, 1 (Vatican II).

40. *The Rite Thing*, pp. 78-83.

41. Karl Rahner, *op. cit.*

E. A. Sovik

The Place of Worship:
Environment for Action

It may be curious to start a discourse like this by telling you what it might have been if I had taken another road in the course of preparation. Nevertheless, I do want to let you know there is another path that would lead to about the same place that I expect to reach in thirty or forty minutes. And it is an interesting road, especially for students of architectural history. I could have started by noting the almost complete absence of church buildings in the first three centuries after Christ, observing the surge in the years after Constantine during which radical changes came to the church, tracing the development of Christian temples to the marvels of medieval times, looking at the variety of things that happened and didn't happen to buildings as a result of the Reformation, and examining the Ecclesiological Movement of the nineteenth century which contributed so very much to the forms and attitudes which are our immediate heritage. And then I might have traced the currents of reaction that began to appear a couple of generations ago, the creative thought, architectural and liturgical, that has been moving us back toward a position more consistent with the postures of primitive Christianity. And then I could have proposed the reasonable future toward which history seems to be moving us.

But I am not going to take that path. Instead, I want to examine the issues related to building environments for worship as an architect and also as one who wants to be a follower of Jesus. As I have said, this road seems to me to converge with the other. Both lead us to changes of real consequence that may be disturbing or satisfying, and are surely challenging.

The buildings we construct perform a double function. They are tools which help us accomplish certain utilitarian objectives, by providing shelter and facilities; this is one function. For another, they inevitably become symbols or images. As such, they reflect, echo, articulate, concretize our ideals, hopes and visions; and they also help to establish among us those ideals, hopes and visions. If church buildings are faithful and lucid images, they have the power to form and reinforce the Christian attitudes and understanding among us; if they are false images or confused ones, they can corrupt or deform us; and since buildings last a long time, they can deform our children too.

So when we prepare to build the environment for worship, we need to start by examining what we believe, and what kind of agreement of mind and spirit it is that brings us together. Then the images or symbols we erect may be faithful to the truth to which we are committed. This being so, I want to start by saying some things about the way Jesus and his followers define the religious life.

Defining the Religious Life

All religious people confess the divine, a transcendent, infinite, ineffable and awesome mystery under whose aegis our bourne of time and place has its being, and seek to open themselves to the encounter with the divine. But there are two ways of responding.

One sort of religion tends to separate from the remainder of life the response to the divine. Its proponents categorize the religious, and separate it from other human enterprise and experience. The encounter with the transcendent for what we may call ceremonial religion takes the form of rites and rituals which are often of great complexity—rules, interdictions, theologies of immaculate precision and elegant complexity. Religious life and thought doesn't seem to connect with the rest of life and with what is called the secular world.

The rituals and regulations often seem even to be antihuman. The frequent form of ritual that develops is the sacrifice in which a valuable thing is destroyed; and the most extreme form of this activity is the human sacrifice, a ceremonial that seems terrifying to us. Even though this particular ritual may no longer be known, ceremonialists are far from unknown, and a good deal of what they do participates in the antihuman character. Christians have been found on this side of the fence; consider the concern of some altar guilds that church candles should be 51% beeswax, or some of the discussions of medieval scholastics. The scribes and Pharisees of Jesus' time were ceremonialists. There was an argument between two famous rabbis in those days about whether it was permissible to eat an egg laid on the Sabbath.

Ceremonialism seeks the divine encounter through esoteric activities which are the bridge between God and man. Because they are so important, special places are built for the rituals. These places are called temples or shrines or houses of God. And just as religious ritual is separated from other human activities, and is called sacred, so the places also, the temples or shrines, are sharply separated from the secular or profane world and are called sacred.

The other direction religious people can go is quite different. The numinous or transcendent is not necessarily attached to the esoteric, but is seen as ubiquitous. God is present everywhere. The religious encompasses all human life. The presence of the divine is recognized not only in the strange, the magnificent, the exotic, but in the familiar and the common. The wonder of the holy is found everywhere, as immanent as the beat of the heart and the rhythm of breath. The *mysterium tremendum* is seen in the "flower in the crannied wall." The whole world we live in can be recognized as "a country that is not our own," as Wallace Stevens said.

In this kind of religion there is resistance to fixities, formulas and rules. Religious activity is seen as that which benefits the life of the world and human life. Righteousness, humility and love are intended to be pervasive and controlling factors of religious life, which is all of life. The encounter with God is not governed by certain times or places; it can be continuous. No shrines or temples are needed because people are themselves the temples where God dwells.

Jesus and the Ceremonialists

Now there isn't much question about what kind of religion Jesus taught. He was the archenemy of ceremonialist religion. He couldn't get along with the scribes and Pharisees. Jesus' repudiation of ceremonialist religion angered them and they ultimately found him intolerable. It is frightening to reflect that inasmuch as we are ourselves ceremonialists—as we all tend to be—we are ourselves one with the scribes and Pharisees.

There is no record that Jesus ever took part in temple worship; and it seems to me inconceivable that if he had done so it should not have been recorded. In contrast to those who thought the temple important, he said to the Samaritan woman that worshipers need neither Jerusalem nor Mt. Gerizim.

He didn't need any special buildings for his ministry. Once on the Mount of Transfiguration when Peter proposed to build some shrines to memorialize the place of that epiphany, he said, "No." And once when he came to the temple and found that the court of the Gentiles, which was intended to be open for everyone, had been taken over by the adjuncts of ceremonialist religion—the sellers of sacrificial sheep and doves and the moneychangers—he chased them all out. He attended synagogue meetings and preached there, it is true; but they were places for teaching and common prayer. Teaching, preaching, healing and cleansing were the essential acts of Jesus' ministry, not ceremony and ritual. The story of the rending of the temple veil at Jesus' death teaches with undeniable clarity, I should think, that such a thing as a separated, sacred place is not a possibility for Christians.

The Era of the Early Church

The practice of religion in the early church was consistent except, possibly, for the short-lived community of Judaizers centered in Jerusalem. Nowhere in scripture do we have any evidence that Jesus' disciples built or wanted to build a house of God. The early

churchmen met where it was convenient to meet; the presence of
God among them was warranted by their presence, not by any
quality of the place where they met. Because they had no temples
and no special places of sacrifice, some people alleged that they
were atheists. For they alone, among the many religious peoples
and cults in the Roman Empire, had neither temples nor altars.

It is conventionally supposed that the reasons that Christians of
the first three centuries built almost no houses of worship were
that they were too few, or too poor, or too much persecuted. None
of these is true. The real reason they didn't build was that they
didn't believe in ecclesiastical buildings. For Christians, as the
church fathers (echoing the New Testament writers) said repeatedly—Christians are the temples of God. His presence is where they
are, and the Christian religion finds its fundamental expression in a
life of love and human concern, the reflection of God's love and
his concern. Christians were known as the community who loved
each other. Their behavior was exemplary, and there is evidence
that the Roman magistrates who sometimes persecuted and killed
them did it reluctantly and were troubled by the injustice of their
actions.

Ritual and Ceremony

What then about ritual and ceremony? If Jesus and his early
followers repudiated the idea of special places or temples, did they
also abandon all ceremony and ritual?

No, indeed not. But there is a distinctive difference between the
rituals of Jesus and the early churchmen, and those of ceremonial
religion. Just as Jesus' parables were images that sprang out of
ordinary secular human experience, so were his rituals. They are
close to ordinary life, and might even be called secular rituals.
Once when a woman anointed him with a fragrant oil, which was
a secular ritual, he contradicted the disapproval of his disciples. He
approved of the ritual. He agreed to be baptized by John in a ritual
derived from the cleansing bath. The eucharist develops out of the
domestic meal, and in the early church was apparently part of a
community dinner. An event that supplies nourishment to the body

is enhanced by prayer; and in this ritualizing of an ordinary meal, the meal becomes nourishment also to the spirit.

So ritual is not abandoned, but ritual has a different sort of position in Jesus' religion. It is a sort of formal articulation of the religious reality that God is close to all of life. It is a sort of work-of-art in which truth is clarified, given formal expression, remembered, illuminated—a celebration of reality. Ceremonies are not the reality of religious life; the reality of religious life can exist through all of life, every moment and every place. Ritual is the formal recognition of this, the intensifying of this awareness. It makes sense to say that ritual is not religion, it is the celebration of religion.

A birthday party is a revealing parallel. The year passes whether we have a party or not. But the birthday party is a secular ritual that takes note of the year and celebrates its passage. So just as it is only reasonable to celebrate a birthday when there is a reality behind the celebration, so it is only reasonable to enact the Christian rituals when there is a real faith and a real community and a real life and a real commitment, to celebrate.

I think that our traditional patterns of designating certain places to be houses of God, and building into them a kind of special ecclesiastical character to separate them from secular architecture is wrong. I think it is unfaithful to Jesus' position and that of the early churchmen. And I think it only proper that we should make a radical change in what we have been doing. I think we need to depart from many of the practices and attitudes that have been conventional in the establishment churches since the time of Constantine in the fourth century, and graft on again to the posture of Jesus and the early church.

The Nature of Celebration

What this means in a really practical way forms the bulk of what I have yet to say. But before turning to this matter I want to make some necessary comments on the nature of human celebration. For even though I will agree that the meaning of Christian worship is not exhausted by calling it a celebration, it is both an ancient and a very illuminating practice to think about worship as celebration. And we can learn something by looking for awhile at secular celebration.

In secular life we don't usually provide permanent places for celebration at all. We use places that are planned for other purposes and convert them into places for celebration. We do this by using all kinds of temporary devices: bunting, banners, balloons, crepe paper, flowers, torches. And the celebration is accomplished through a whole series of other ephemeral, transitory and temporary things, processions, firecrackers, costumes, gestures, speeches, music and singing, eating and drinking. This is the way we celebrate outside the parish; it is fruitful to observe that some of these elements are the core of our worship celebrations too. It is not the ecclesiastical building, replete with permanent devices of bronze or stone or stained glass that makes the celebration; it is the music and song, the speech and gesture, the candles, flowers, bread and wine—things that come and pass away, are consumed, completed, abandoned. It is to accommodate these things that we have to provide an environment, a place for actions—not for things.

There is another characteristic of celebrations that is pertinent to our concerns: Those secular celebrations like anniversaries and birthday parties, which recur in cycles, are always built on a skeleton of ritual. The birthday party, for instance, always has the cake and candles, the gifts in their throw-away wrappings, the food and drink and the song. But every good birthday party is also in some way different from every other; those who plan the best celebrations know that they are better if there is some surprise, so they invest some imagination and creativity.

Christian worship also has a skeleton of ritual that we call the "ordinary," and there is provision as well for the changeable which we call the "propers." And a fruitful worship celebration is one in which the fixed and expected is supplemented by the fresh and new.

Furthermore, as Fr. Debuyst elaborates in his fine little book *Modern Architecture and Christian Celebration,* it is always the presence and participation of people that makes a celebration good. All this is to remind you of something you know already, that authentic worship doesn't depend on having a permanent, ready-made, completely detailed and decorated place, but on people and their action. All of us have had the experience of profoundly effective worship services in *ad hoc* places, in the woods, on a lake shore, in homes, and other places not specifically designed for worship.

Indeed, as we reflect on the matter, I think we must come to the conclusion that it is really better for Christians not to have places that are specifically and exclusively built to be places of worship. Such places inevitably tend to stabilize, fix and stultify the forms of worship. There is too great a temptation to let the building and its artifacts control the liturgy, and there is too small an opportunity for the imagination and thoughtfulness of those who plan and perform liturgies. But the more important reason is that inevitably, if we build the kind of places we have generally been building, they come to be thought of as houses of God. Inevitably God's presence will become associated with a structure and its furnishings. The building will accrue to itself the qualities of a temple, and the Christians' consciousness that they are themselves the temples will be diminished. History is absolutely clear about this. The record of what happened after Constantine to the church at large, and the records of what happened among Mennonites, Puritans, Methodists and others who began their institutional careers without church buildings is very convincing evidence.

To Build or Not to Build

Now I want to turn to the practical issues. I think we must not build any more churches. By churches I mean, in the first place, structures which are designed specifically about their programmed use as places of worship; and in the second, structures which seek to identify themselves, through design motifs of one sort or another, as places separate from secular architecture, and thereby suggest a degree of special sacrality.

If we are not to build such places, what shall we do? Shall the churches disavow building altogether, as the early churchmen generally did, and find places to meet wherever they can? I think you will agree that this is indeed a viable path. And there are, in fact, a good many congregations across the country who have taken this path, and are content that it is the right one.

But a couple of assumptions made by those who have gone this direction may turn out to be illusions. One assumption is that it can be a permanently effective approach; in fact it is very difficult for a parish to avoid some sort of building if it grows much and undertakes to do many things. The other assumption is that the funds that parishes invest in structures will in this sort of building-less parish be spent in other more worthy service. It is very difficult to generalize on this, of course. Some records we have of the early church indicate that the building-less churches of Rome in the middle of the third century did pretty well. About 40,000 Christians were able to support with their charity 1500 people. On that basis a parish of 400 nowadays ought to provide a minimum of $30,000 for charity each year! On the other hand, a denominational official told me recently that of 23 new parishes established during a recent year, one had decided to be a parish without a building, and this one was 22nd on the list in per capita giving.

Some congregations who have initially taken the no-structures route have found it necessary to abandon it. In this day and age it does appear to be impractical. The automobile with its requirements for parking space makes trouble. The practical size of our parishes and the smallness of our homes makes meeting in homes awkward, and other gathering places may be unavailable. Furthermore if a congregation wishes to be a servant in a community, its capacity to serve is enlarged if it has the tools of service; and buildings, as I said earlier, are tools for service. Parishes who refuse to equip themselves to serve cannot serve. So there are good reasons why parishes most often find it mandatory in these times to erect structures.

If we accept this alternative, that assumes the erection of shelters, we face the question, "What shall we build?" and even before that, "For whom shall we build." Dr. Edward Frey gave one answer at a conference in Washington some years ago. "No congregation ought to enter a building program at all," he said, "if its intent is only to serve its own needs." The church is the servant of the world. As Jesus was the man-for-others, his followers must be men-for-others. And the building program ought to start with a study of how a congregation can find ways to serve the needs of the general community.

Consider a "Centrum"

In most communities one of the needs will be a place of assembly—a space or room which can find alternate use as a gathering place for the worshiping congregation. Such a room will not be called a "church." It has always been a mistake to call buildings "churches" anyway; the church is a body of people, the community of believers. The place may be called a meeting room, or a hall, or we may find another name. Let us use the word "centrum," because it is a secular sounding one.

If such a place is to be a really useful tool, it should be a place of extreme flexibility. Let me describe what kind of characteristics this implies in my mind. The shape of the floor area will not be very far from a square. A simple square or circle or octagon or other regular shape is possible, but probably not wise for acoustic and other reasons. A rectangular shape is not required and the room need not be a clear-span open space; but of course any complexities of shape or structure need to be weighed for their effect on whatever variety of uses is anticipated and against their cost.

The floor almost inevitably will be flat, though some terracing may be possible. Galleries may be useful in large centrums. The room will have no strong axial character, so that a variety of configurations of people and furnishings can be comfortably used. This may imply asymmetry. And there will be no dominating focus established by structure or the shapes of the containing walls or vault or ceiling. The latter will be of a height appropriate to variable uses, large groups of people and esthetic considerations.

Daylighting needs to be cautiously designed to avoid glare (colored glass may be a useful factor serving this intention), and to serve daytime needs. Artificial lighting ought to be general and there should be resources for a changeable variety of special lighting devices. If the room is large enough to require a sound system, its elements should be movable. Ideally, the acoustic character of the room may be made variable through the use of devices such as are frequent in concert halls. Equipment for projecting visual images, still or cinematic, ought to be provided, possibly rear screen projection, since this technique doesn't require darkening a room.

This is a fairly short summary of the utilitarian qualities of a centrum. Some comments are in order about the furnishings also, and the first obviously is that a minimum of the furnishings (perhaps none) should be fixed in place or too heavy to be moved. Clearly this means chairs, not fixed pews: There is a number of good interlocking, stacking or folding chairs available on the market now.

Practical needs will inevitably, except in small rooms, require a platform, and like the seating, it should be movable. Logic says that it should be made of modular units that can be moved and arranged in various patterns for various uses. Such modules can be good looking, durable and light enough.

There will be some special items of furniture required for any non-cultic use of the centrum, and when it is used as a place of worship, some specifically liturgical equipment will be needed. All of it, the table, pulpit, candlesticks, fabrics, cross, utensils, symbolic devices and accessories need to be portable, as portable as the equipment in the Israelite Tabernacle. I confess there is something attractive to me about the image all this portability provides—the image of a pilgrim community that moves in and out of the sheltering centrum. It is the people, and these artifacts which serve their actions, that make of the centrum from time to time a good place for worship.

I believe I should say something about the arrangement of a space for worship, because although there are many ways of organizing a free space, there are some ways that are better than others. The first thing—and this is probably familiar to you all— is that we must get rid of the nave/chancel syndrome. The body of Christ is one, not two. Worship is not a matter of audience/

performer; everyone is a participant, no one is passive. The whole room ought to be seen as chancel, if we want to use that word at all anymore; there is no nave.

The typical arrangement of laymen all facing one direction toward a stage-like chancel is really corruptive. A congregation is something like a family, if we want to use a scriptural image, and worship is something like a family reunion; in such an event people ordinarily arrange themselves as if they like to see each other, in a circle or a horseshoe, not in ranks like strangers in a cinema.

To break down the audience/performer image several things can be done: First, the furniture should not be so arranged as to imply a sort of heirarchical importance, which happens, almost inevitably, in symmetrical arrangements. Instead, no object should appear to carry much importance except when it is in use. Second, any sharp distinction or distance between the people and the various foci of liturgical action should be minimized; this is one of several good reasons for getting rid of the communion rail, which always seems like a fence. Third, as much as possible, the arrangement should work toward mixing of liturgical action, people and artifacts or symbolic devices. For instance, flowers or candles need not all be banked around the altar; they might be many places in the room. The cross (which if it is portable is likely to be on a staff) or banners (if they are used) need not be close to altar or pulpit; they can stand out among and around the assembly of people.

The choir ought to be located where it can sing well, and we shouldn't be troubled if it is very visible. One sort of acoustic virtue often accrues in a choir gallery, but there is an offsetting fault if the choir is unseen. I can't think of a circumstance except in our churches where serious music would be performed by singers who are behind their listeners.

Architecture as Image and Symbol

I started a few paragraphs back to talk about the centrum as a tool, but I have been talking also about symbolic values of the furniture and its arrangement.

I want now to shift clearly to questions of architecture as image and symbol. How does a Christian community express through the way it does things the truth about the way Christians understand themselves, God and the world? As I have said, the structure an institution builds always becomes the symbol of the institution; we can't escape this. So we must take seriously the urgency that our symbols be both faithful and lucid. And what I have left to say will focus on the symbolic character of architecture. I might start by saying that it is absolutely inadequate to mount a cross on a building, no matter how big, to apply biblical inscriptions to it, or to use any of the other familiar devices by which we recognize the conventional church building. These devices are simply labels, and as we all know, the label has no necessary correlation to reality.

A man doesn't need to be much of a Christian to wear a cross on his lapel or a woman a cross on a necklace. The real evidence of Christianity is whether they express themselves with integrity, whether they act with love, and whether they live in the continual consciousness of the presence of God.

A building that represents Christian people needs to exhibit these three qualities too. If a structure has integrity, it will display a kind of wholeness, consistency and unity, which is one of the meanings of integrity. It will also avoid every affectation, every deceit, dissimulation, imitation and artificiality. This means that a building has really to be what it appears to be. No historical styles, of course. No imitation marble, no quarter-inch plywood v-jointed to look like solid boards, no steel beams cased to look like timber, no electric candles, no plastic plants, no electronic bells. Formica and the other plastic laminates are fine, but not if they look like linen or wood. I don't mind a bar-room Hammond, no one mistakes it for a pipe organ; but when an organist tells me his electronic sounds exactly like a real pipe organ (which it may), I think, "Where is your integrity?" The better the imitation is, the more surely Christian people should reject it.

If we are to worship in spirit and truth we can't surround ourselves with the phony and ersatz. And if our lives are to be lived with integrity then *all* we build, whether a place we use for worship or anything else—but certainly the structure that is taken to be the image of the Christian community—all we build ought to be real. We should be reminding ourselves that the gospel story starts with the incarnation; God enters the world in a village stable. If this is so we have no need for exotic and opulent palaces. Our buildings—not only our centrums, but all the structures that Christians build—should be authentic, earthy buildings, because the gospel says God enters the real and uncosmetic world.

A Hospitable Environment

An environment that properly represents a Christian community needs also to be an expression of love. The words to describe this kind of structure are not easy to find, but possibly the word "hospitable" is as good as any. Our buildings ought to be at least as hospitable as our homes; kind, gentle, friendly, open, comfortable buildings that accommodate themselves to people.

There are lots of the other kind of public buildings, as we all know, and a great many churches are among them—pompous, ostentatious buildings that seek to be imposing and important; buildings that dominate people rather than honor them, impressive monuments, images of power and authority. The church has been caught up in this pattern long enough, as if the gospel were some sort of authoritarian imposition rather than the gift of love and forgiveness.

To build an environment of the character implied by this ideal is one of the most difficult problems for an architect. The issue is not whether a building is large or small; it is a question of how it relates to the human being; and it involves that most elusive of all architectural factors—the thing called scale. It involves the other sensible factors, too—color, texture, rhythms, light, space and sequences of spaces. I will say no more here than that the best architectural designers are necessary; people with high sensitivities and skills, whose minds are not set on building monuments and grandiose architecture, but on providing hospitable places for people.

If one needs a special skill and attitude to provide hospitable places as a reflection of the Christian ideal of love, he needs equally the rare gifts that can provide adequately beautiful places. The urgency of the beautiful is based for me on the understanding of the relationship between beauty and the perception of the transcendent. Christians ought to live in the constant awareness that their whole existence is encompassed by the tremendous mystery of God. And ideally, as the Christian takes responsibility for giving order to the world about him; he ought to be saying to himself, "I want to provide the kind of order, the kind of shapes and spaces, the kind of total environment that will be a continual reminder to people, no matter what they are doing, that the ineffable, transcendent, awesome, fascinating mystery of the divine is immanently present."

Let me say again that although we are sometimes brought to the condition of wonder when we are in the presence of the strange and magnificent, it is wrong to suppose that the sense of the numinous is attached only to the exotic and the opulent. We also hear this "trumpet call from the hid battlements of eternity" when we reflect on the most intimate and ordinary things. And of human enterprises, the one that most often stirs within us the sense of the numinous is the work of the artist, the beautiful thing. This is because beauty, like holiness, is impossible to rationalize, analyze or synthesize. We respond with wonder to both. The beautiful thing is, I think, the only symbol we humans can devise that illuminates the transcendent.

This is the reason the priest who deals with the holy and the artist who deals with the beautiful have always been companions in every religion. And the reason we ought to build beautiful places for worship is not that "nothing is too good for God," but because the work of art can help men to remember that they live in God's country, a country of the ineffable mystery.

The Nature of Beauty

I want to bring you some reminders about the nature of beauty, that I think are useful when we deal with the environment for our worship. For one thing, beauty is not a matter of decoration.

There isn't anything necessarily wrong with decoration, but a beautiful thing doesn't have to be ornamented. A good axe handle is a beautiful thing and ornament would probably ruin it. There are many beautiful spaces without ornament, too.

Nor is beauty a matter of novelty or strangeness. A good deal of architecture these days—and this includes a great many so-called modern churches—is an attempt at novelty or excitement. It tries its best to be "interesting." Beautiful things are never dull, to be sure, but buildings that depend for their virtue on simply being new or different lose their novelty after awhile, and we come to think of them not as beautiful but merely bizarre.

Beauty is not a matter of self-expression. There is a certain kind of designer or artist whose aim is to put the stamp of his private vision and personal preference or prejudice on all his work. This process is sometimes called creativity. But beauty is discovered, not created, as truth is discovered not created. And though we want an artist to work from conviction, his commitment should not be to himself, but to a vision beyond himself.

Now that I have said what I think beauty is not, I trust you won't expect me to supply three paragraphs on what it is. But I will give you a famous sentence that has been nourishing me for a long time. It is St. Augustine's definition. "Beauty," he said, "is the Splendor of Truth."

I have spent these last minutes talking about the beautiful thing as the image of the transcendent with careful purpose. So many people when they speculate on the possibility of abandoning the tradition of church building in favor of secular and multipurpose places like a centrum, react with pain or rue, supposing that this must mean the knell of fine architecture and the submission to dull and commonplace structures. I hope that what I have said is enough to indicate that this is the furthest thing from my mind.

But we must not go on as the ceremonialists in history have done, building carefully and elaborately for places of worship, and not troubling too much about the secular or profane environment. We are constrained to do more. We must accept the secular as the ambit of God's presence; and this leads us to two consequences. First, we can worship appropriately in environments of secular character, because God can be there. Second, we must, as far as we can manage it, make our whole environment and all our structures into forms that are images of what is good and true and holy. This is a heavy burden, but it is what Jesus asked for.

Daniel B. Stevick

Renewing the Language of Worship

I do not know what you expect in a paper on "renewing the language of worship." Perhaps another go-around on "you" vs. "thou" in prayer. Perhaps comments on whether the tone of prayer should be chatty and casual or distanced and measured. I regard the rhetoric of liturgy as important and discussable. I have expressed some opinions on it elsewhere. It is agenda for a seminar of this conference.

But for this paper I have other themes in mind. I hope you will not think them less important. The crisis of worship, insofar as it is a crisis of liturgical language, is not only a technical matter of word choice and sentence organization. The call for the renewal of language and style goes much deeper. Concern for language cannot be separated from concern for what the language refers to. There is a theological, hermeneutical problem that is basic. Amos Wilder has recently called for a "theo poetic"—an investigation of theology, faith, and liturgy as dealing in the stuff of imagination. Worship—as communion with God and an interpretation of existence—depends on a fabric of images. The pictures in our minds impart meaning, carry authority, create community, move to action, and suggest the reality of all that is beyond here-and-now experience. Such pictures are not merely decorative. They are a primary mode of apprehending reality.

The trouble is that the convulsions in today's society confront us with a crisis of the word, a disruption in the immediate accessibility of essential, time-tested images. Wilder again has put it: "What we are going through can be seen as a crucible of language, a crucible of images, a testing and transformation of signs and symbols, a revolution of sensibility" *(The New Voice,* p. 24). Insofar as worship depends on the acceptance and believability of a large, coherent body of images, it is deeply threatened by the kind of transformation of signs that Wilder describes. Liturgy is a fragile structure of acts, words, and images; and it can seem vulnerable today.

"Renewing" Is a Hopeful Word

I find two implications in my assigned subject: (1) Talk of liturgical renewal expresses weariness, a sense that worship is dealing in tired words and forms. No one spends time discussing the renewal of something which is satisfactory as it is. (2) Anyone who considers the language of worship to be capable of renewal must assume that the terms of liturgy are at least partially in our control. We do not have to accept them as they are. We do not have to stand by as today's crisis of metaphor destroys the ingredients on which worship depends. We can take them in hand and refashion them. "Renewing" is a hopeful word. Some creative fresh departure is possible, is required by our situation, and can be expected.

I think that convictions of this sort—though they are far from universal—are widely shared in the Christian community. It is not merely that strange things are going on around us—old practices are being abandoned (apparently with little regret), and experiments open new possibilities. It is also the case that strange things are going on within us. Forms and words and styles which seemed acceptable, adequate, and self-validating—and at moments glorious—until a short time ago rather suddenly seem to show their age. Terms and ways which ministered life seem weary, stale, flat, and unprofitable. Hymns, psalms, and prayers which we have used with gratitude in corporate exchange with God now seem exotic—elements from someone else's world, speaking for someone else's inner life. We pause (Or, lest I put words in some-one else's mouth. I should confess that I pause) and ask, "But can I say that? If I can, is it mine if I say it in this way?"

The Problem of the Words

The words of worship are, to some extent, no longer doing their job. They have become problematic. They should go un-noticed. We should not say, while we are at worship, "What impoverished words!" or "What effective words!" The terms and forms of worship should present to us—so far as public words can suggest it—the measureless wonder and glory of God. They should express, illuminate, and enlarge our human experience. They should mediate the corporate encounter of God and his people. But now they call attention to themselves. We find our minds drawn to the means, not the end. It is like listening to Bach when the organ starts to cipher, or a violinist when a string breaks, or an important speech when the sound system begins to crackle. We become preoccupied with the thing whose main purpose is to direct our attention to something else. A medium which should be transparent has become clouded.

The problem is serious—serious for the church, for worship, for the faith. We cannot fall back on the many persons—tens of thousands—who feel little of all this and who use old words and old thought forms with continuing satisfaction. We cannot assume the crisis will pass. Our primary apprehension of God is by way of images. When we pull away from an inherited body of words and symbols which for generations has intimated, so far as language can, the mystery of God, the problem is not casual. Liturgy's own primary questions have been raised.

What has brought about this drawing-away from past words, past images, past styles? No change in taste, ideas, sensibility, cultural climate is easy to explain. But I suggest three factors which have introduced real discontinuities between us and our devout ancestors:

Worn-out Terms

First, the terms of worship were allowed to become routinized and stale. Most terms of worship arise first as an original apprehension of the reality of God. Someone, in the depths of his soul, sees something new, and he finds a term that clarifies it for himself and communicates it to others. Some such sharp, richly perceived terms have perpetuated themselves for a long time. But the church is an institution of fixed habits. Communities go on using forms and words long after the impulse that gave rise to them has faded. Manners of speech, bits of phrase, structures of thought go on after any outside critic would recognize them as conventional and over-extended. Their work is done; they should be given a graceful retirement. Yet hymn and prayer and preaching continue as a tissue of cliches. No first-hand experience is required; one can do all his thinking and feeling in derived phrases. The reality of God—reaching into human existence to shatter and rebuild—can be held at a distance by forms which are not validated freshly or criticized.

It is reasonable to assume that the persons who coined the vocabulary of liturgy or who first put its material into English speech or who gave a creative impulse to enduring forms of worship did so out of something freshly seen, freshly responded to. But certainly the tendency of most traditions, in time, is towards a safe, comfortable bourgeois idiom that cannot radically judge or redeem. Our heavy touch makes liturgy dull and prosaic. Within our familiar forms, we grow self-indulgent or sentimental. We introduce the banalities of children, mothers, country, benevolence, or the self-glorification of the institution. Or else we betray some desperation by stunts, shows, tricks, and fads. Great worship must derive from a great gospel greatly apprehended. But too much worship in the modern era has committed the ultimate heresy of presenting a Christ who is reduced and dull—not worth the trouble of crucifying or of confessing as Lord.

This is (or so it seems to me) the first of the factors that has pulled us away from the inherited terms of worship. Most of the traditions of worship in the modern world have become decadent and self-imitative. Their creative days are behind them.

The Chasm of History

But a second factor is that important historical discontinuities have come between us and the basic terms in which theology and worship have classically expressed themselves. The metaphors from the tradition of liturgical speech are only partially usable. Some images of man-under-God are elemental. They are derived from birth, growth, marriage, suffering, and death, or else from natural observations of water, the sun, distance, and the like. Their meaning remains recognizable over the centuries. Even these, however, are modified when we hold birth, pain, age and death at a safe, antiseptic distance. What happens to the wonder of light and the terror of darkness in an age in which light is available at any time by the flip of an electric switch? Darkness is not a mystery pressing upon us; we can dissipate it in an instant by an intentional act of our own. We are the creators of light. What happens to the sense of the Spirit of God—the *ruach Elohim*—in an age in which people do not live in the desert, in tents, exposed to the wind and its sudden cessation? Some artificiality and shelteredness has come between us and these basic images. Yet they remain relatively familiar and understandable.

But many of the most significant characterizations of God which have dominated the devotional and liturgical tradition derive from social, cultural, and religious patterns which are much more distant. A great deal of our worship and hymnody gathers around four circles of images: king and subject, shepherd and sheep, priest and sacrifice, father and child. For their effectiveness, these images depend on backgrounds in absolute monarchy, in herdsman culture, in ritual defilement and animal sacrifice, and in patriarchal, autocratic family—all of them, for most Westerners, dead for a considerable time.

The church is a strange community. It carries within it words and pictures in the mind from a distant era, and it shares these words in its liturgical speech as though they remained accessible and expressive. Consider one such picture. I once heard a devout friend remark that the greatest text in the Bible is "Behold the Lamb of God who takes away the sin of the world." I do not know how anyone would determine what text in the Bible is the greatest, but if the criterion is that it gather up important, pervasive threads, this one would be a contender. But the image "lamb of God" does not at once impart a clear meaning. It emerged from a shepherding people—a people whose fathers and heroes, Abraham, David, Amos, had been shepherds. It emerged from a background of lambs as ritual offerings for sin and restoration of communion with God.

The temple cultus would have suggested that an animal might have something to do with taking away sin. The mysterious Suffering Servant figure is described in sacrificial terms; God's own sacrificial person was dimly foreshadowed. Thus when someone first said of Jesus "Behold the Lamb of God who takes away the sin of the world," the terms had immediacy and force. It was shocking and not necessarily convincing—only faith could make it that. But its terms were comprehensible. It was gospel. The true sacrifice for the restoration of the race had been made, not by man, but by God. "The Lord will provide himself a lamb."

Over the centuries great tracts of Christian hymnody, art, and devotion have developed this picture—Christ the sacrifice, the paschal offering, his blood shed for offenders and their cleansing. Take this body of material out, and a quarter of our hymns and our eucharistic piety would crumble. A great communion hymn established itself within the high moment of sacramental action: "O Lamb of God, that takest away the sins of the world. Have mercy upon us."

Now the question I am asking is what meaning this image has for urban, technological man. What can the lamb of God mean for my two million neighbors who live in God's own asphalt, who know a lamb only as an exotic wooly creature in the children's zoo, and who if they heard that anyone were going to kill one for a religious rite would call the S.P.C.A. I do not say that the thing the image signified is unimportant or irrecoverable. But I point out that the cultural, social, and religious background that interpreted these words is gone—and gone irretrievably—for most persons in today's world.

In general, modern culture has taken decisive, irreversible steps away from a number of the categories and images which have expressed the ways of God and carried the basic symbolic language of worship and devotion. Words that have conveyed a sense of God—his character and his redeeming action—to Christians over many centuries increasingly convey nothing at all, or else a meaning other than their original. We shall not deal adequately with the crisis of liturgical language until we are prepared to look honestly at the loss of many of our classic terms.

Of course, ancient terms and the thought forms they imply can be learned, like any specialized vocabulary, and used by an in-group. But does not the use of culture-bound terms tend to locate the divine reality itself in the past? And does not a spirituality which can only speak to God in dated terms suggest that it is infected by a false nostalgia or a delusional remoteness?

Moving Into New Worlds

But, to turn to a third item, it is not just that old experience and old language are no longer available to us. It is also the case that we move into new worlds—worlds in which we live, think, and feel—and which as yet have no adequate place in liturgy. Modern life is propelled into new modes of experience by technology. But the important thing for us as worshippers is not that we drive automobiles or watch television. Rather it is that we perceive things differently; we live in a different world; we move at a different rhythm and pace; we organize our communities differently; we define ourselves and our neighbors in different terms. New experience has been opened to us by romanticism and anti-romanticism, by science and its revolutionary account of our universe, by psychology and fuller self-knowledge, by art and new ways of looking around us. We are moved by considerations that were, in many cases, not conceivable a few generations ago. And it would be possible to go to church Sunday after Sunday and not find liturgy making any significant use of the rich experience of the life of today. I live—I live deeply, richly, interestingly— in today's world, struggling to be humane and responsible. Yet in most of the worship that I participate in, I am expected to put aside my contemporary existence and adopt the identity of another people.

Perhaps I can illustrate the feeling by an account from a fine book of a few years back. In Sylvia Ashton-Warner's *Teacher,* the author tells of her class of Maori children in New Zealand who were learning to read. She cites some of the conventional printed material which explained that the child "can be led to feel" that the comings and goings of the children in the textbooks could be made important to themselves. Miss Ashton-Warner asks "Why try to lead a child to feel that these strangers are friends? What about the passionate feeling he has for his own friends?" The child is already full of intense fears, angers, attachments. The joy of reading should come through putting a child in touch with the deep reaches of himself—naming the unnamed, unmanageable stuff of his experience. With this conviction, the teacher discovered a word of vital meaning for each child—she called these "key words"—and wrote this word on a card, told the child it was his word to have and take home. The words were organically related to the powerful inner life of the child— "Mummy," "Daddy," "kiss," "frightened," "ghost." The next day each child would bring his dog-eared card back and get a new word—vivid, sharp, and his own. His vocabulary would grow. No word was forgotten. The child was using his reading to establish some meaning within the maelstrom of his inner life.

Isn't that something like what many people are feeling is missing from worship? The characteristic words of worship are other people's words. An alien vocabulary is imposed. We are singing other people's psalms and hymns, declaring the meaning of faith in other people's creeds, speaking to God in other people's prayers. One doesn't want to be too shrill. Surely old words, images, actions, and forms can be important witnesses to the continuity of human life. In much of this ancient, distanced, formal material, a worshiper can recognize himself and find illumination of his existence. But where, in all of it, is the "key word" vocabulary? What use is made of the things that move us? Where are the words of immediacy and power that spring from the depths of the struggle of contemporary life? Perhaps, like Miss

Ashton-Warner's schoolchildren, we should come to church with cards in our hands—cards bearing the words, phrases, half-formed ideas, that express the inquiries, discoveries, failures, joys, anxieties, hopes of the week past. Perhaps the agenda of worship should be composed from this material. Some liturgical genius should gather the cards at the door and weave expressive worship from the secrets they utter. As it is, too little in worship brings into play the words which have been forged in the intense experience of our own time—the words which have become powerful, evocative, authoritative, and liberating. A profound hunger is not fed; a rich resource goes unused.

The Problem of Control

But it is just the necessity of that liturgical genius that brings up the other side of the matter—the problem of control, of theological center and organization. So far I have been presenting considerations that make us and our contemporary experience the standard and which call into question terms and forms that belong to other people in other times. I would contend for this element. It has been underrepresented. Worship has been formulaic, general, and remote, even in the freest traditions. But worship is not just an account of our experience in appropriate words. It is an opening of ourselves to the God of revelation. The church is not just a community which shares its common experience, it is a community which remembers Jesus Christ. And Jesus Christ is only available to us on his own terms, as living Lord, in one context— the witness literature of the Bible. And the Bible is only available to us in one context—the faith community which has read it, believed its message, interpreted it, and lived from it. When Christians assemble, they are a people with a history and with an account of themselves that roots in a redemptive act of God. There are, in other words, *givens* which are constitutive of life and liturgy. The integrity of the words of worship cannot be measured by criteria from today's culture and speech alone. The integrity of the words of worship ultimately depends on the faithfulness with which they represent the Word. The Word declares itself. It authenticates itself; nothing else can authenticate the Word. Liturgy is tested by the adequacy with which the worshiper is presented with that living, powerful, ordering, gracious self-utterance of God.

The basic words of worship do not come from contemporary self-awareness. They come with a history—the history of persons engaged with the Word. We are not free with respect to them. They are, on our lips, a covenant with past moments of disclosure and with the company of those who are in Christ before us. "Others have spoken, and we have entered into their language." These basic terms—reaching us from history—bring to modern experience and its one-sided self-knowledge a point of interpretation beyond itself.

Oddly, it is often just those craggy, dated, offensive images from the past—king and subject, shepherd and sheep, priest and sacrifice, father and child—that we find we cannot do without. They touch and open a range of experience that modern images seem not to reach. They give depth and adequacy to our sense of the tragedy and the redemption of which the gospel speaks. Modern innovations have not fared well. Images of storm-tossed ships and safe harbors (many of them developed in seafaring Britain, but sounding rather precious in the Midwest where I first heard them) seem anthropocentric and sentimental. Images of trains, radios, and the like, which one hears occasionally, are contrived, not discovered. Certainly the conditions of modern life provide materials in which the Christian imagination can find images of God in action, as Jesus saw them in everyday life of Palestine. But the new images are tested by a gospel which has been given in other images. The old, difficult images from a bedouin, pre-scientific, pre-industrial, pre-behavioral studies age keep reasserting themselves. The old, with all their difficulties, remain the criterion of the new.

Martin Buber once spoke passionately for the old terms and the load of significance they bear. As he tells it, someone had commented to him on the terrible misuse of the word "God." To speak of the highest by that often-defiled name almost seemed blasphemous. Buber replied to his friend:

"Yes, it is the most heavy-laden of all human words. None has become so soiled, so mutilated. Just for this reason I may not abandon it. Generations of men have laid the burden of their anxious lives upon this word and weighed it to the ground; it lies in the dust and bears their whole burden. The races of man with their religious factions have torn the word to pieces; they have killed for it and died for it, and it bears their finger-marks and their blood. Where might I find a word like it to describe the highest! If I took the purest, most sparkling concept from the inner treasure-chamber of the philosophers, I could only capture thereby an unbinding product of thought. I could not capture the presence of Him whom the generations of men have honoured and degraded with their awesome living and dying. I do indeed mean Him whom the hell-tormented and heaven-storming generations of men mean. Certainly, they draw caricatures and write 'God' underneath; they murder one another and say 'in God's name.' But when all madness and delusion fall to dust, when they stand over against Him in the loneliest darkness and no longer say 'He, He' but rather sigh 'Thou,' shout 'Thou,' all of them the one word, and when they then add 'God,' is it not the real God whom they all implore, the One Living God, the God of the children of man? Is it not He who *hears* them? And just for this reason is not the word 'God," the word of appeal, the word which has become a *name,* consecrated in all human tongues for all times? We must esteem those who interdict it because they rebel against the injustice and wrong which are so readily referred to 'God' for authorization. But we may not give it up. How understandable it is that some suggest we should remain silent about the 'last things' for a time in order that the misused words may be redeemed! But they are not to be redeemed *thus.* We cannot cleanse

the word 'God' and we cannot make it whole; but,
defiled and mutilated as it is, we can raise it from
the ground and set it over an hour of great care."
(Eclipse of God, pp. 7f.)

Between Old and New

I have tried to set before you the claims of the old and the new
that describe the liturgical situation. The church is a community
of oldness and of newness. We are Abraham's children, wanderers
of the ancient Near East. Yet we belong to today—its grandeur and
its misery. God has spoken in historical events. But he speaks to
judge and redeem in every present moment.

We utter the words of Christian worship with an accent modified by a varied past: patriarchs, psalmists, prophets; evangelists,
apostles; fathers, martyrs, councils; mysticism and scholasticism;
Reformation, Counter-Reformation and sectarianism; rationalism
and pietism; missionary zeal and social reform; theologies of existence, process, secularity, hope, and revolution. We are present in
every past and distant in every present.

We are under two claims—neither of which, as I see it, can be
dodged. Both derive from the gospel in the church. We cannot
yield to either to the exclusion of the other.

Yet this is a hard saying. By temperament, most of us are drawn
more to oldness or to newness. You probably have heard the claims
of either tradition or contemporaneity pressed within the week.

These two claims are both rooted in the gospel itself. One asks
for faithfulness to a redemptive event and the images which are
bound up with its significance on its own terms. The other asks
that we have confidence that that moment is not confined to a
point in time or a cultural formation from the past, but it can be
declared livingly and contemporaneously as the redemption of every
moment. These two claims, in their force and tension, run some
risk of immobilizing, dividing, or compromising the church. Unfortunately, when it comes to liturgy, most official commissions try
to do some justice to both. They halt between two opinions. They
give a little here and take a little there. They trade off a little

oldness for a little newness. The effect on liturgy seems rather like a classic utterance:

> "Oh, help!" said Pooh. "I'd better go back."
> "Oh bother!" said Pooh. "I shall have to go on."
> "I can't do either!" said Pooh. "Oh, help *and* bother!"

We get able, responsible worship commissions trying to take account of a Christian community which is going very rapidly in several directions at once! Whatever the result may be, it is hardly the renewal of the language of worship.

No rules for liturgical speech can be prepared in advance. A new kind of excellence is being sought for which no model now exists and for which old models may be misleading. The concrete experience of a language community precedes the fashioning of guidelines. Excellence emerges and is recognized as such. The account of the qualities of that excellence (facilitating its imitation) comes later.

We cannot at this point anticipate what direction liturgical speech will take; it is likely that we will be caught by surprise. What we can do in advance is to ask of ourselves *on the highest theological grounds* that liturgical speech be good speech. We can be confident that the crisis will call forth its own answer. New terms, styles, manners of liturgical speech will emerge—perhaps of several kinds. But to say what will be accepted as good language for worship a few years from now is, in my judgment, beyond the best of us.

But I think it is possible to say where we are just now and why prediction is difficult.

Culture builds up its forms around the felt questions of life. While those forms are stable, there is a correspondence between our inner and outer worlds. Culture is ordered so that it answers our deepest questions. Culture evokes in us the questions it is able to answer.

Such a stable period can be enduring and productive. But this stability breaks down. People arise who ask different questions and who do not find existing forms life-supporting. Such a period is marked by disorientation and anomie. The ground rules which have ordered the world so that it can be lived in confidently are under question. The common assumptions that bound community together no longer hold. The alienated individual is on his own. In such a period of transition, there is much waste and fragmentation. Many possibilities are opened which prove unproductive. Many good people cannot adjust to that which is coming into being. They remain isolated and embittered.

But such a period is also a time of discovery, potentiality, innovation, and exhilaration. Great it is then to be alive, and to be young is very heaven.

Liturgy is not primarily a cultural form. On the believing account of the matter, worship is a gift of God. But it always expresses itself incarnationally—in the cultural forms of time and place. It evidences its continuity and self-identity from age to age, not by absolutizing any specific form, but by adapting, with the confidence of faith, its basic actions in the new forms that emerge when culture changes. When new existential experiences call old structures into question and require new patterns and new words— "Liturgists, *sursum corda!*"

Observations at the Turning Point

We are obviously at a massive cultural turning point now— probably the most significant transformation since the Renaissance. I offer three observations:

(1) Have you reflected on the enormous liturgical creativity of our time? The general forms of worship that we have been using have persisted since the 16th century—though the roots of all go back into Christian antiquity, of course. Most liturgical thought has been antiquarian. Old models defined the possibilities. Catholicism was bound by rubricism and juridicism. Except for its bursts of hymn writing, Protestantism has been uncreative. Restrained by official regulation or by the grip of custom, worship has changed only within narrow limits. "As it was in the beginning, is now and ever shall be, world without end."

But we have quite abruptly moved into what seems to me to be an unprecedented period of experiment and creativity. Not all of the experiments are equally good. Much well-intentioned impulse seems superficial. Yet, has there ever been a time in the history of worship when so much was going on? This period of innovation is an ecumenical phenomenon. It is not defining the differences between the Christian bodies; it is taking similar forms everywhere. It is being participated in by parishes, monasteries, and informal groups, above ground and below. No elite is making things happen; no central authority could make them stop. Most church bodies are asking for intelligent participation in the process of change by whole, diversified memberships. Architecture, song, visual media, community, ceremonial actions, as well as speech patterns are involved. The whole *gestalt* of worship is changing its look and sound. Many people seem to be hoping that all of this will soon be over; they think it is time it all settled down again. But I for one think it is a kind of release which has not yet produced its best work. It would be a tragic mistake to try to shut off this creativity prematurely. The Spirit is speaking to the churches. The time in which we live is, to my mind, one of the most exciting and hopeful moments in the history of worship.

(2) The Christian community in this period of creativity badly needs a sense of self-criticism. It has always seemed that one of St. Paul's wisest practical observations was that the gift of tongues should always, in the public worship of the church, be paired with the gift of interpretation. Whatever style of utterance might be acceptable in private, St. Paul judged that the common life required "edification," building up, by the intelligible word. In a somewhat analogous way I think of this time of release and creativity in the church as requiring a more than ordinary discrimination, control, and testing. There is a risk that whatever is done in the service of devotion will be indulged beyond its merits. Sincerity and piety are not adequate aesthetic touchstones. Hasty, unexamined work is too much in evidence. At the same time that new material is becoming available in a flood, we need an ongoing conversation about criteria for judgment. We need theoretical categories to give coherence, discipline and force to material that often emerges in bits and scraps. Theological discourse on the means and ends of worship has never been more necessary. The gift of spon-

taneous utterance is from God, but so is the gift of discrimination.
They need to appear in the life of the church together.

(3) We are at a moment of *kairos*—the judgment of an old era
and the breaking in of a new. Something is dying and something
is coming to life. The church was born in such a moment and
should be familiar with its dynamics. Jesus did not, as I recall, say:
"The time is fulfilled. The kingdom of God is upon you. Therefore be not the first by whom the new is tried nor yet the last to
lay the old aside!" Prudential, pragmatic, political means are not
an adequate transition to the new. We need the spiritual imagination to participate in the desolation and trauma of the loss of the
old but also to venture gladly into what God is calling into being
in our time. We need a new voice in worship, arising from new
people living in a new age. To cling at this moment to the familiar
would risk becoming a religious and cultural backwater. The moment of grace and challenge disconnects us from one past only to
open to us another and a richer memory. But liturgy should not
be occupied with its own past. According to my reading of the
book of Revelation the greatest moments of the creation's worship
of God are not those which have been but those which will be.
Liturgy should be oriented to that coming, cosmic celebration. Our
task and joy in worship is to stand within our present, shaped
inevitably by our past, and in this place to make as audible as we
can a song which is going on now, and always will go on—a song
to one we know by an ancient and troublesome yet luminous metaphor: the Lamb.

Wayne Saffen

Worship
and Political Responsibility

Worship is the political act *par excellence.*

This recognition may come as a rude shock, accustomed to thinking (as we are) that worship is one thing and politics another. We have come to think popularly that religion is one thing and life another, political oratory one thing and public preaching another, political corporate expression one thing and Christian assembly another. This popular thinking is undergirded by ecclesiastical and theological arguments. It also wears many veils of self-deception.

The grounding of this attitude in the United States may be found in the "absolute wall of separation between church and state." It is grounded in the Bill of Rights, that no [single] religion shall be *established* in our society by law.

The popular opinion is undergirded by many Lutherans, moreover, by the doctrine of the "two kingdoms," and "left and right hands of God." This dichotomy becomes easily a split between soul and body, private and public, political and religious, this-worldly and other-worldly relations, secular and sacred. Such distinctions may be made on paper and even in logical thinking, but rarely in life, private or public, personal or social. It is schizoid thinking which leads to split personalities and mere role playing in social functions. It distintegrates the integrity needed to keep persons whole and integrated.

However, this Lutheran doctrine of two kingdoms grew quite understandably out of its medieval catholic context of trying to resolve the conflict between religion and politics with the formula of the "Two Swords"—papal and imperial. That whole concept, in either its Roman or Lutheran formulations, was shattered upon the steel of Adolph Hitler's *Wehrmacht* and the introduction of the idea of a totalitarian state, a new god on earth laying total claim to human life.

The emergence of the totalitarian state in the twentieth century his preempted the place of God in human consciousness and obedience. The modern militarized state is omnipotent, omnipresent, and omniscient—if not holy, good, gracious, and kind. It is essentially idolatrous when it defers to no God above it, recognizes no rights of conscience, requires unquestioning obedience, recognizes no "Law above the law."

For citizens, it becomes idolatrous (in Luther's understanding of idolatry) when it evokes supreme love, fear, and trust. It moves religion to the private sphere, determines the limits of its public functions, approves and disapproves which religions shall be tolerated. It encourages religious support of the political liturgies and conventions and persecutes religious opposition to political rule. If popular religion is caesaropapistic, as American religion tends to be, no conflict is seen. If religious support is lacking, the state develops its own religious trappings of public worship.

Some Examples

First, the modern corporate state acquires the status of god on earth. The basic concept in the modern state is its aspiration to be a "great power." Richard Nixon has made no secret of his feelings of mandate to keep the United States as "Number One" in power. International politics is "power politics." The collective will-to-power is fanned as energy to maintain preeminence. This is the prevailing "national interest" under which any foreign war may be justified if any threat, foreign or domestic, is seen not to the security of the United States but to the preeminence of the United States as the precondition of that security. This power is derived from natural and human resources, from the will to power and patriotism of the people, from the appeal to "our standard of living" no matter what it costs others in the world. It is maintained essentially as a military power. Our "credibility" means that we will, indeed, use nuclear weapons against whole peoples if we feel our "self-interest" threatened. Such a super-power does not rely at all upon God but upon its own resources. Its nearest sense of accountability to God is a sense of history. History is seen essentially as the conflict of great powers, the rise and fall of empires. Its aspiration is to become omnipotent, beyond threat of reprisal, to maintain at least "a balance of terror." The omnipotent state becomes the chief object of fear to men today.

Secondly, the totalitarian state is omnipresent. It extends its powers beyond its borders, maintains armed forces in nations around the world, on the high seas and underwater, in the air and in the stratosphere. Its missiles are pointed at potential enemies around the globe. It maintains its presence in the consciousness of its own citizens and all the peoples of the globe.

Thirdly, the totalitarian state is omniscient. As the media help make it omnipresent, so also its information retrieval systems, computers and intelligence operations tend to make it the repository of all data and knowledge, subject to the interpretation of the rulers at a given moment in history. From filmed records of all public meetings and protests to scanning of bank accounts and IRS returns to telephone bugging and surveillance and political espionage it enters all spheres of public and even personal life. The attempt to get a psychiatric profile of Daniel Ellsberg by burglarizing a psychiatrist's office is but one instance of the reach for omniscience. The psychological pin-pointing of non-conformist kindergarten children as predisposed to criminality is another and larger net.

Technology has made all this possible. It has helped to create the image of the totalitarian state as god on earth, subjecting its citizens to subservience, and setting itself up as the supreme object of fear, love, and trust. As such, the totalitarian state is the perfect idol for our times and its worship is the prevailing form of public worship and idolatry.

Must we reach all the way back to Isaiah to subject Leviathan to ridicule? (Isaiah 40). Or to the Psalmist?

> The idols of the nations are silver and gold,
> The work of men's hands.
> They have mouths, but they speak not,
> They have eyes, but they see not,
> They have ears, but they hear not,
> Nor is there any breath in their mouths.
> Like them be those who make them—
> Yea, everyone who trusts in them! —Psalm 135:15-18

In looking underneath the trappings of the technological totalitarian state, we discover that it is human beings who worship power who demand worship of themselves in the abstraction of the state. This worship has become a marked feature of modern totalitarian states. Hitler, Stalin, and Mussolini were crude representations of the elevation of "Fuehrer" into idol worship as personification of the state. Franco and Peron were others. But so, also were Roosevelt, Churchill, Eisenhower, Kennedy, Johnson, and Nixon. In our own lifetime, worship of the charismatic individual who personifies the national will-to-power has become transmogrified into the worship of the institution as such and automatic respect for whoever presides. Soviet reaction against Stalin resulted in a rejection of "the cult of personality," for the interim, at least. China has yet to go beyond its worship of Mao Tse Tung, since he is still with us. Uniquely, The Committee to Reelect the President, combined projecting the image of Richard Nixon as president with the virtual obscuring of the man. George McGovern complained that he did not get a chance to run against Richard Nixon, the man, but The President and his surrogates. The very words of idolatry are used in the packaging of all candidates for public office, with chief concern for the "image" they project. This so-called "Christian nation" has come to worship image and finds reality almost impossible to cope with. Politically, socially, and (I fear) religiously, image has come to take the place of reality in the public and personal consciousness. This is the quintessence of idolatry.

When the masks come off, we find it is actual human beings who manipulate all levels of power, presence, and intelligence. They return to lifesize and the idolatrous form of the state is seen to be mere mechanics for purposes which are not divine but human. We will look in vain for holiness, justice, mercy, goodness, kindness in anything like deified proportions in these fellow human beings like us all in every way. When we apotheosize human beings we lay impossible burdens upon them and delude ourselves into impossible expectations. Then we rage at the gods who fail to meet our expectations. Since this is a matter of idolatry, we can destroy the gods we make. This discovery enables us to get at where gods come from. It is too easy to scapegoat the humans we make into idols. For we are the idolaters.

"The human heart is an idol factory," said Martin Luther.

The collective will-to-power produces the national idols. This idolatry is actually self-worship, identified with the nation, the history, the ideology, the party, the man, the apparatus, the system, the way of life, the national interest. Idols may be set up and deposed, elaborated or smashed, gilded or disfigured.

The symbols of idolatry are not easily tampered with without arousing the national wrath. The use of the American flag as an object of worship in the past decade of social strife over the uses to which it has been put in a war which divided the nation is near enough at hand to see how national idolatry works. The flag is, of course, no *mere* symbol, as Paul Tillich said repeatedly. It is not just a bit of cloth. It does represent everything that a country stands for. It does have a place in the heart of our countrymen as a symbol which evokes love of country and patriotism. This is not, in itself, idolatry. It becomes idolatrous when the desecration of the flag becomes tantamount to treason, when it arouses over-reaction and excites legislators to punitive laws, when it is treated as a religious symbol with its desecration equivalent to blasphemy. It blinds countrymen to the uses to which the flag is put, the bad causes in which it may be waved as a guidon, the scoundrels in public life who wrap themselves in it. The flag burnings were not a hatred of the country but in many cases intense loyalty to the country coupled with feelings that the flag itself had been disgraced by what many considered a criminal war. It is clear that such a form of protest did not make its point. The reason it did not is that patriotism had become for many a blind idolatry of the symbols of public faith with loss of perception of the substance of patriotism. The wearing of the flag in lapel buttons and its overuse in decoration cheapened the whole concept of what a flag stands for, particularly when used by partisan political interests against opponents.

It may be seen that the modern totalitarian state which makes itself the supreme object of the people's fear, love, and trust is not simply the product of technology. Nor is it simply the creation of ambitious men. It is founded on that very fear, love, and trust which the people owe to God and give instead to idols of their own making. The modern totalitarian state, inevitably militarized beyond belief, is an idolatrous creation of masses of people who then worship it as real, since it seems to be so and seems to acquire a life of its own. Yet it cannot function at all if popular support is not given and if at every point of enforcement some human being does not carry out his function. It takes no imagination to know that no missiles will go off if humans fail to make them operative, no military will function if everybody sheds uniforms, no taxes will be gathered if nobody collects them, no laws will be enforced unless somebody does it, nor be enacted if legislators will not draft them. At every point some human being carries out orders but is abstracted into the monolith of the national state. It is those human beings in office, as functionaries, and the people who support them, who make the system work, without whom it would collapse. Such a construction of human artifice is patently not God, not even a god on earth. It is only the fear, love, and trust of the people that make it appear so. The totalitarian state, then, takes the form of our collective fears, loves, and trust. It is the image of ourselves we raise to illusions of omnipotence. At that level, the modern totalitarian state is psychologically infantile. Its pretensions at omnipotence will be shattered on the reality of the first NO, which contradicts it and sets its limits. Such a NO is frustrating and triggers anger. Such anger can be dangerous when infantile reactions have technological

means at their disposal. However the NO will be said. It must
be said. If it is not said by the people who worship themselves
in the idolatry of their own systems, it will be said by other
powers who also have means at their disposal. And it will be said
by God who has means at his disposal against which we have no
counterforce.

The Political Fact of the Church

The political fact of the church has been recognized by the
state, if not by the church. The limits of its activities are pre-
scribed by the state and its existence is given charter by the state.
Indeed, religion is offered such special privilege in national societies
that it risks being bribed into silence, aquiescence, and support of
existing social and governmental structures.

To mention only a few obvious points: congregations and
church bodies organize as corporate structures in our society,
registered with the states; the question of exemption of church
property from taxation is a public issue; clergy and seminarians
have been exempted from military service and received tax breaks;
to continue as religious non-profit organizations they must specifically state they will not engage in political activities; whether
or not Jehovah's Witnesses must salute the flag or serve in the
armed forces is decided by the supreme court; the question of
financing religious education with public money is a matter of
public debate and law.

There is almost no stir when prominent churchmen lead Sunday services at the King's Chapel in the White House but the
seeming public advocacy by churchmen to evade the draft or
desert military service, if that is dictated by an aroused Christian conscience, is prosecuted in courts of law. Some religious
speech is free; others are not. This is not at this point an argument on the merits of either case. It is simply to note that some
religious expression gets official approval when it agrees with
public policy and suffers official wrath if it opposes public policy.
Opposition to public policy may be tolerated up to the point where
it becomes effective. At that point political rulers may praise a
Billy Graham or a Norman Vincent Peale while indicting a Daniel

Berrigan, James Groppi, or William Sloane Coffin. Nor is it at all problemmatic where the nation of sheep lines up. They follow the political leader. The majority is invoked and the prophetic churchmen are brought to book in court.

This is not to ascribe malevolence to the American political structure. It is simply to say this is how it is and this is how it works. It is highly susceptible to malevolence or benevolence on the part of elected rulers. At any rate, the role of religion in public life is not determined by the churches but by the political establishment in consort with public opinion. Public opinion increasingly is formed less by religion and more by politics, culture, business, and the media. It is easy to see the difficulties Christians have in public worship in countries which are openly atheistic and anti-religious. It is harder to see in the so-called "free world," until a Martin Luther King arises in the United States or a Bishop Dom Helder Camara arises in the right wing Brazilian military dictatorship.

The political fact of the church has been recognized by both church and state since its inception. The Old Testament church was a religious and political entity, with priests and prophets. Prophecy was the uniquely biblical mode of self-criticism for the religious and political communities. "Because no prophecy ever came by the impulse of man, but men moved by the Holy Spirit spoke from God" (2 Peter 1:21). Both the religious and the political communities were on notice that they were subject to God's judgment and that God would send men to speak the truth, whether either community wanted to hear it or not. That is what it means to have a word of God. The attempt to suppress the word of truth, the word of God, in both the church and the state happens at that precise moment in human history when earthly powers seek to escape God's judgment and punish the messengers who bring the bad news to the king. It is a behavior so repetitive among men of bad faith that Jesus scored his opponents who glamorized their own history:

> Woe to you, scribes and Pharisees, hypocrites!
> For you build the tombs of the prophets

And adorn the monuments of the righteous, saying
'If we had lived in the days of our fathers,
We would not have taken part with them
In shedding the blood of the prophets.'
Thus you witness against yourselves
That you are sons of those who murdered the
      prophets.

—Matthew 23:29-31

The church was a political fact of life ever since the days of Jesus. He was crucified under Pontius Pilate upon the official charge of setting himself up as king of the Jews and stirring the populace throughout the whole country. He was charged also with threatening the central symbol and visible institution of Jewish religion, the temple. He was charged with blasphemy, making himself out to be God. He was condemned officially by the legitimate power structures of his time. He was declared a political criminal outside the protection of the law.

Every one of Jesus' disciples was persecuted and prosecuted by the state. Most were executed as enemies of the people. Some were mobbed and stoned and beaten with the police standing by watching it happen without interference.

The Roman persecutions are well known and the martyrs celebrated in the church. Who martyred them? Why were they executed? Why were Christians deemed enemies of the state, subversives? Why would they not burn the pinch of incense to Caesar, a seemingly simple loyalty oath? Caesar knew and Christians knew then, though many may not know now. Christians were willing to obey the state and honor the emperor, but not as God. Caesar was not God on earth. Nor was he even Lord, although he was a lord. Christians recognized Jesus, ascended to heaven, as Lord of lords and King of kings. This political defiance of the totalitarian rule of Caesar was recognized for what it was: the breaking of all totalitarian claims of any state on the allegiance of Christians and of all human beings.

The Bible celebrates the faithful worship of God in the very face of political repression. Daniel opened his windows and prayed to God in the sight of all in direct defiance of the law which prohibited it. The faithful would not bow the knee to Baal, emperors, Caesar or to any worldly power as God on earth. They would not be silenced and they would not evade the confrontation with any constituted authority which demanded of them that worship which belongs to God alone. In more recent times, Martin Luther would stand before pope and emperor and refuse to yield his obedience or deny the word of God or his own conscience. In every age faithful Christian witnesses have taken this hard line publicly. The eleventh chapter of Hebrews is redolent with cases of men of faith who refused to capitulate to earthly usurpation of the place of God.

The conflict of powers on earth which we call power politics and which seem to make up history is met with a Power beyond all the powers in the church. Christians open our Lord's Prayer saying: "Our Father who art in heaven." The creed issues its defiance to all the great powers: "I believe in God the Father Almighty, Maker of heaven and earth. And in Jesus Christ, His only Son, our Lord." Every communion is a public act of remembering the Lord's death, his body given and his blood shed for us. "As often as you eat this bread and drink the cup you proclaim the Lord's death until he comes" (1 Corinthians 11:26). This is a political act.

The political fact of worship is that it recognizes God as ruler over all, heaven and earth. It reduces all earthly powers to temporality within the limits of his will. God establishes powers and he overthrows them. They come, and then their day is done. The only reason a Christian would be subject to any earthly power at any given time is because he recognizes that God is in it working out his own designs quite independently from whatever the great power thinks it may be doing.

Christians worship the Power beyond the powers, the presence of God in Christ, the free movement of the Holy Spirit quite beyond any power of human beings to limit, the living Word of God which leaps out of the opened Bible to almost any given situation, the will of God which is done without our prayer, his kingdom which comes with or without our effort, the Word of

God over any word of men, the Law of God in the face of all human statutes, the allegiance given to God above and beyond all human authorities and despite them when necessary. We recognize God as Spirit whom we worship in spirit and in truth, quite beyond the ability of any human authority to control, proscribe, or limit.

Every act of public worship is public notice of the fact of first allegiance to God, the recognition of Christ as Lord sending the Spirit of Truth as the power of God to lead us into all truth. The Christian church is one, holy, catholic, and apostolic. That is a political fact. It transcends all political boundaries, all national boundaries, all historical boundaries. It is a fact in history, a witness to God's rule among us, his salvation, his right arm made bare and the victory over death won by Christ, the power of perfect love in Christ to cast out all fear. The attempt of every society to nationalize its religions is an attempt to nationalize God and to destroy the catholicity, unity, and apostolicity of the church. We will not permit that to happen, since no national power has that authority. Every public worship and every confession of the ecumenical creeds is a political act of renunciation of every religious nationalism and of every national religion.

Jesus opposed the totalitarian rule of religion over the life of human beings: "The sabbath is made for man and not man for the sabbath." So, in our day, we must oppose the totalitarian pretensions of any national state, ideology, or culture over the lives of human beings ransomed with the blood of Christ from every bondage: The state is made for man and not man for the state. That is a political act.

How Can This Be Done?

Following the lead of Martin Luther's mode of questioning in his catechetics, it may be transparent that we move from questions of "What does this mean?" to "How can this be done?" We move from dogma to pragma, from faith to works, from word to act.

This is no easy shift of gears. The supreme court of the United

States has limited what it considers to be free speech. In so doing, it limits "speech" to words and excludes acts from constitutional protection. This is a patent judicial effort to limit the communication of meaning. The supreme court may declare this erroneous theory of words and communication but it has no power to enforce it. That is to say, the ability to enforce this theory of speech can succeed only if people substitute words for all acts, if all prohibited acts are foresworn and avoided, if people talk instead of live. Life would have to be lived vicariously for this theory of human communication to succeed.

Suppose that we were to say that we may talk about the Lord's Supper but not actually eat bread and drink wine. If there were a rule against alcoholic beverages, communion could be proscribed by law. Such attempts have indeed been made. The church will not yield. Talk about communion is no substitute for it. Indeed, St. Paul says: "As often as you *eat* this bread and *drink* the cup you *proclaim* the Lord's death till he comes." This is an act which speaks. It goes beyond words. Its mere doing makes its point again and again through all of history. We are not about to suspend the practice. We do not need to, since at present there is no law against it and no political urge to suppress it. But such was not always the case, is not now in every country, and may not be for us in the future. Suppose its political significance were raised to a heightened consciousness in the Christian community. Suppose its import would be understood to the public at large and to governmental circles: that in the communion we celebrate the rule of Christ as our risen Lord, that thereby we confess him as Savior of the world, judge of the whole world in history and at its end. Suppose a favorite hymn would not be seen as innocent at all but as explosively political: "Beautiful Savior, Lord of the nations, Son of God, son of man, Truly I'd love thee, truly I'd serve thee, light of my soul, my joy, my crown." This hymn is perfectly harmless unless we mean it. A lord who does not rule, who has no subjects, is no lord. To claim citizenship in his kingdom, however, and to recognize Christ as Lord above all earthly powers is a political act of incalculable consequences. It sets Christians in conflict with any activity of the totalitarian state which usurps

God's prerogatives of worship or exclusive and prior claims on any Christian's allegiance to any fatherland.

The public worship of God is that political event which recognizes the rule and sovereignty of God over all. Christian worship recognizes Christ as Lord of history and of the world, not just of the church. Specifically, Christ breaks down the wall of separation between nations, between classes, and between sexes (Galatians 3:28). This is not simply a matter of private belief or a religious tenet of a particular group. It is a claim upon the world to be voiced through the church by public proclamation of the law and the gospel. It is the kerygma, the basic message to be preached to the whole world. Preaching and evangelism are to be as public an event as the crucifixion. To have preaching relegated to church in the pulpit on Sunday morning in an inoffensive service for those who like that sort of thing short-circuits the message. It is an attempt to limit the free course of God's Word in the world.

To be sure, religion has gone public in its building programs, the airwaves are full of preachers, and television lets ministers sign off. The latter are standard butts of ridicule for Johnny Carson and late night talk shows. Religion in public life cuts no ice. It has no edge. It has an incredibly low level of expectation. Discipleship, the discipline of being Christian, yields to the more pressing disciplines of making money, filling out forms, doing study assignments, training for sports, military preparedness. The Word of God is effectively blunted by being so muted (even when shouted into a microphone) that it lacks specificity in any interstice of human life.

It is quite another thing to lay a draft card on an altar, to collect and burn draft cards in church, to have a public procession on Good Friday making places of human suffering and injustice stations of the cross, to go on a freedom march in Selma, Alabama, confronted by troops at the end of a bridge, to attempt to exorcise the Pentagon, to picket the White House, to appear at national political conventions. Television cameras zero in, along with secret police and official surveillance. When the Word of God is read from the Bible speaking directly to public issues, the heat goes on. In congregations, pastors lose their pulpits if they speak out on public issues. More than one minister apologizes for his lack of prophetic courage and adopts the priestly role, not realizing that all the political dynamite is loaded in the ordinary liturgy and lections and eucharist of any given Sunday.

It should be clear that worship is tolerated so long as it is non-political and irrelevant, the specificity of the Word suppressed, the worshipers narcoticized against reality. As if to prove Marx right, we make religion the opiate of the masses to keep them from becoming conscious of Christianity's revolutionary import. Our doctrines are trimmed to meet prevailing political ideologies, to maintain privilege and place in a society where victims get preached at and powerful interests are left unscathed. No Nathan arises to confront the president with the charge: "Thou art the man." The deference to earthly powers is so complete, the church so abject and subject, that it may be questioned if God is indeed its own object of worship and confession. Christ gets named into innocuousness, while his radical claims to our discipleship get reduced to mere lip service. It has become a mystery to most contemporary Christians why anybody would have crucified Jesus. He was such a nice man, the crucifixion seems unreal. Equally hard to understand is why the church was ever persecuted. Who would want to persecute a nice bunch of harmless people? We think the age that crucified him must have been different from ours, so blind are we to our own times and the crucifixions going on all around us. The national flags occupy our chancels as if they were objects and symbols of the Christian faith, along with the altar, cross, and candles. Worse yet, we sense no conflict. They seem to belong there. The church has become subservient to the national religion and interests to maintain its privileged status. Its own political nature has become so obscured that it is no longer seen.

Lutheran worship concentrates on Word and sacraments.

The politics of this worship is to arouse, develop, and maintain a God-consciousness which transforms human thinking from the cultural concensus to Christian confessionalism.

Preaching has the potential of confronting minds formed culturally with the Word of God which breaks like a hammer, cuts like a two edged sword, penetrates and changes hearts, brings Christian thought into conformity with Christ. It is a radical tearing down of presuppositions and building up a whole new way of seeing things. It opens eyes and ears to see what is there and to hear what is really happening. It tears off the veils of delusions until reality emerges bare faced. It confronts people with the electric vivid voice of truth. The Word of God is read, explained, proclaimed, spoken until people see what it says. Usually the words need no explanation. Indeed, we may spend most of our time explaining them away, lest their radical force be felt. Hosea, Amos, the psalmist, Isaiah and the prophets generally are so specific, it is no wonder they are rarely heard in the churches. Pastors say, "The people aren't ready for it." At the current rate of soporific homiletics, they never will be. Preaching alone could almost carry the load, if we dared.

But set in liturgy, combined with an understanding of Baptism as dying to old ways and rising with Christ into newness of life in this very world, and the regular celebration of Christ's resurrection from the dead in Holy Eucharist is a political act which can only be understood as insolence to the powers that be who threaten sanctions against nonconformists. The whole liturgical service is itself a political act which challenges all assumptions of any would-be totalitarian state or self-sufficient culture. It proclaims Jesus Christ as Lord and bends the knee only to God.

Introduce drama as part of special preaching services, let the songs of protest and affirmation be sung in church, take worship out into the streets and public assemblies, juxtapose popular beliefs directly to clear words of scripture, upend parishioners from their pews and spill them into participation, utilize role playing devices, let the imagination roam free, and everything becomes alive.

Christian worship of God in Jesus Christ by recognition of the Holy Spirit who calls, gathers, enlightens and sanctifies us by the gospel is the political act *par excellence.*

The fault is not in the liturgy. It's all there: from the invocation of the Holy Trinity (invoking God's *Name*), to the kyrie (proclaiming Christ as Lord), to the psalms and lessons and epistle and gospel, to the sermon, to the creed, to the offering (our bodies as living sacrifices), to prayers which acknowledge God as the Father of lights (stars) and giver of every good and perfect gift, invoking his rule over all nations and our own rulers, to the sanctus (where we veil faces with cherubim and fall down before God, proclaiming that he alone is Holy and the whole earth is full of his glory), to the benedictus (Blessed is he who comes in the name of the Lord), to showing forth the Lord's death as a political criminal until he returns, to the final blessing, the whole liturgy is a public act of political proclamation of our Lord and our King.

The fault is not in the Bible. It's all there, everything about human nature and sin and society, about politics and empires and wars, about rule and order and overthrow of governments, about laws and order and chaos, about official injustice and oppression, about vested interests and tainted wealth, about kings and priests and prophets, about scribes and pharisees and zealots, about whores and tax collectors, about drunkenness and carousing, about the high standard of living which is maintained by oppressing the poor, about freedom and slavery and self discipline, about obedience and disobedience, about authority and love and action. The open Bible has become a closed book because it is rarely read and gingerly preached. A willful ignorance is encouraged, in spite of all the high geared teaching, to blunt its radical claims.

The politics of the Bible is a politics of liberation. This is what God does in Christ. It is what he does in history. It is explicit in Mary's *Magnificat*. God demonstrates and establishes his righteousness, forgives sin, and makes us truly righteous in Christ. The Light has come to light up the whole world. To reduce this Word incarnate in Jesus and explicit in the Bible to mere words recognizes the potency of the politics of worship. This is the good news of liberation and redemption in Jesus Christ which the church is called to represent and proclaim. It is the fundament of the Christian confession.

> In the presence of God who gives life to all things,
> And of Christ Jesus who in his testimony before
> Pontius Pilate made the good confession,

I charge you to keep the commandment unstained
    and free from reproach
Until the appearing of our Lord Jesus Christ;
And this will be made manifest at the proper
    time by the blessed and only Sovereign,
    The King of kings and Lord of lords,
Who alone has immortality and dwells in
    unapproachable light,
Whom no man has ever seen or can see.
To him be honor and eternal dominion. Amen.
                —1 Timothy 6:13-16

That is a political confession *par excellence*. It is confession of faith. It is worship and acknowledgement of God. No truly political person who worships the totalitarian state would miss its point. It is instantly clear. It is an unequivocal political statement. It is the usual language of the Bible, when worship proclaims the political facts of life as Christians see them.

No evangelistic blitz is needed to win the continent to Christ. Such a campaign is foredoomed to failure as just one more media blitz to package an image of God and Jesus and church to make them acceptable to the people. If nothing happens in worship or preaching or Christian confession or Christian life as witness, no ad campaign can change the fact of unbelief. When the worship comes alive it will be experienced as political in the conflict it engenders in every participant who refuses to give the worship due God alone to an idol as substitute. The political fact of that worship of God alone in Christ will have consequences in all our lives that none of us can escape. The problem is not that we do not know this. The problem is that we do. To avoid the conflict we enervate our worship, dull our senses, mitigate the scandal of the cross, sentimentalize our hymns, and get excited about Watergate after being quietistic about Vietnam. And then we wonder where God went in our world and how to get people back into church, as if that were our problem.

The churches will indeed empty out when people discover that worship is the political act *par excellence*. They will wonder why we talked so much about the cross and never told them about it. They will have the feeling we never really levelled with them on what the Christian faith was all about. And they may be right.

When public worship is raised to the level of political consciousness as being Christ's disciples in the world, preaching without fear or favor, and confessing God against all secular totalitarianisms, going to church could get interesting again. There is, in fact, no better way of turning people on to what it is all about. We Christians might even get excited again about being in on God's great conspiracy to save the world, a secret hid for ages and still closed to those who consider it foolishness or who are scandalized by the execution of that political criminal we confess as Lord of lords and King of kings, proclaiming his kingdom come to overthrow all kingdoms, his rule over all, his grace for the world's salvation, his body and blood our pledge, his cross our sign of faith, his return to judge the whole world in righteousness, his Holy Spirit even now at work in the church and in the world through all the visible and invisible means at God's disposal.